Catriona Mackay

Effective Marketing

In easy steps is an imprint of In Easy Steps Limited
4 Chapel Court · 42 Holly Walk · Leamington Spa
Warwickshire · United Kingdom · CV32 4YS
www.ineasysteps.com

Notice of Liability
Every effort has been made to ensure that this book contains accurate and current information. However, In Easy Steps Limited and the author shall not be liable for any loss or damage suffered by readers as a result of any information contained herein.

Trademarks
All trademarks are acknowledged as belonging to their respective companies.

In Easy Steps Limited supports The Forest Stewardship Council (FSC), the leading international forest certification organisation. All our titles that are printed on Greenpeace approved FSC certified paper carry the FSC logo.

MIX
Paper from responsible sources
FSC® C020837

Printed and bound in the United Kingdom

ISBN 978-1-84078-426-8

Contents

Customers, competitors & all that jazz

Marketing is not an event, but a process... It has a beginning, a middle, but never an end, for it is a process. You improve it, perfect it, change it, even pause it. But you never stop it completely.

Jay Conrad Levinson

First of all, a little jazz!

What exactly is marketing and who does it?

To save yourself any unnecessary brain ache, there are already many widely accepted definitions of marketing and so it's worth ensuring you can roll one or two off your tongue, should the occasion require it!

The Chartered Institute of Marketing defines marketing as "the management process responsible for identifying, anticipating and satisfying customer requirements profitably."

"Marketing is the social process by which individuals and groups obtain what they need and want through creating and exchanging products and value with others." – Kotler

Probably the easiest to remember and the most commonly used by marketing students is "The right product, in the right place, at the right time, at the right price." – Adcock

Anyway, good marketing is about satisfying customer needs, now and in the future. However large your company, sole trader to multi-national, everyone should be focused on meeting the customer needs, wants, and requirements.

Why do you need it?

To get bigger, of course.

You need effective marketing if you want to grow your business in a thoughtful and sustainable way. For example, good marketing will ensure that all the functions involved in your business are able to work at their best level of productivity.

Manufacturing will be able to make the correct number of widgets to meet demand, sales will be able to sell those widgets for the best possible price, customers will be delighted and continue to buy from you as you introduce new and exciting products. Like a conductor at the front of the orchestra, it is your job to make sure each musician plays at his best and the result is harmonious!

What it is not...

Marketing is not about selling as many poor quality products to as many unsuspecting customers as possible. It is not about creating a hullabaloo about a product or service, which cannot live up to the hype. Nor is marketing about developing products, which seem like a good idea based solely on the enthusiasm of staff.

Don't forget

Marketing is not something you pay attention to for only a few minutes of a day.

Marketing is also not something you pay attention to for only a few minutes of a day or fit in between 'real' work. Nor is it a black art, only to be mentioned in hushed tones!

The place to start is ALWAYS the customer

Now if you want to raise the level of the conversation, you could introduce a little philosophy of marketing and quote the greatly respected guru, Peter Drucker –

"Marketing is not only much broader than selling, it is not a specialized activity at all. It encompasses the entire business. It is the whole business seen from the point of view of the final result, that is, from the customer's point of view. Concern and responsibility for marketing must therefore permeate all areas of the enterprise."

Don't forget

The customer is always right.

That will probably bring any light conversation to a rapid close! Mind you, by the time you get to the end of this book, I hope you'll see exactly what he means... Your aim should be to become a truly 'customer-centric' company. This is important because if you understand what your customers want, you can deliver the best products or services to them. Satisfied customers will come back, again and again.

Knowing your customer

Imagine your whole customer base is an orange. You can speak about the whole orange with broad statements, such as:

"It's large."

"It is orange."

"It has a waxy feel."

"It smells tangy."

But peel the orange and suddenly you have so much more to see – look at the variety of sizes, flavors and texture in the segments. Now we can really start talking!

That may not be the most exciting metaphor but bear with me. Think of your customers as one group (or a whole orange!) and you can probably make a number of generic statements. These might be true but will be so broad that they won't be much use if you wanted to make someone really feel familiar with your customers.

Marketers are like Santa Claus!

You have it in your power to make customers happy! All you have to do is ask the right questions and act on the answers...

For instance, imagine that when asked for a Christmas gift list, you just answered in generic terms ("a CD", "a car", "a bottle of perfume"). Chances are you'll not receive exactly what you want despite the good intentions of the present giver.

However, the more detail you can put down on your list, the more likely you are to receive the perfect gift. As a consequence, the present giver is also thrilled when they see your delighted reaction as you tear off the paper, screaming "It's exactly what I wanted!"

Segmentation

As you answer the questions below it will become obvious that your customers (or potential customers) are not one homogenous group but actually a number of distinct groups (or segments) with individual needs.

Where to start

Ask yourself (and your team, if you're lucky enough to have one) the following –

Hot tip 

Create personalities for your customer profiles – draw pictures of them and put them on the wall.

1. Where do they want to buy?
2. How do they want to buy?
3. When do they want to buy?
4. What other products/services do they buy?
5. How big is their budget?
6. Will they be making regular repeat purchases?
7. How do they want to hear about our product?
8. What need are we satisfying with our product/service?
9. How many different types of customers do we have?
10. In what ways does each of our customer groups differ?

Targeting

Try to identify the differences between each of the segments in terms of demographics, lifestyles and product/service usage. This will make it easier for you to target your marketing activity on the customer groups to whom your current product appeals.

Good segmentation will also help you to identify the features, advantages and benefits (FABs) future products should offer.

Excellent targeting will save you money!

Your targeting will inevitably be the basis for your marketing communications plan so it's crucial that you can define customer groups who really are interested in what you have to offer. The soggier you're targeting, the more wasteful your communications message will be.

Happy families

It's a good idea to create personalities around your customer profiles – this is one very effective way of identifying your different customer groups. Put your creative hat on and bring your customer groups to life!

Draw pictures of the different types of purchaser (a great 10 min warm up before a meeting for your team can be to use photos and pictures in magazines to make a collage per segment), as these will help you to communicate who your target audience is to the rest of the organization.

Make yourself so familiar with the personality of these customer groups that they come to life for you and your colleagues. Give your characters names. Keep those drawings on your office wall.

It's as if we'd already met

Of course, customers aren't aware of how you have decided to segment them. They should just instinctively feel that you understand what they are looking for from their supplier. Test your segmentation on a group of your customers by showing them your different profiles. If you've got it right, the majority of customers from each segment should identify with the profile created for them.

An acid test of the accuracy of your segmentation is whether the same end user customer appears in more than one segment. If they do, it means that your profiling needs tightening up.

Customer groups all have one thing in common...

Each one is looking for the best possible value they can find!

They do not want to pay for product features they don't want. They do want the product or service to meet their needs. It's a balancing act.

Before you rush off to slash your prices, this does not mean you have to be the cheapest. It does mean that you need to understand what your customers are looking for and therefore what they value. Then you can write a relevant value proposition for each segment. We'll look at this in more detail later in the book when we discuss pricing.

Different sets of challenges

Not only should product features and benefits relate to customer needs in general but to particular segments. In simple terms, the better you are at understanding what customers want, the easier it will be for you to save money by not giving them additional stuff that they don't value!

Now your communications, sales and distribution plans can also be made pertinent to each target segment.

Not all customers are equal

20% of existing customers often account for 80% of your business! It therefore makes sense to be particularly attentive to those who are already worth a great deal to you or who are growing...

You should also consider how many customers you have who are actually worth very little in revenue terms. Perhaps there are better ways to serve them while also taking some cost out of doing business? This will at least protect your profit margins.

Room for more

Remember that you also want to add more good customers to your list. Make it your business to know who the best customers in your target markets are. If they aren't already one of your customers, ask yourself "why not?" What do you have to do to make them want to work with you?

Competitors and indirect competitors

Direct competitors serve the same target market as you with similar products or services; an indirect competitor is a company that serves the same market with different products or services OR a different target market with the same products or services. You must keep an eye on both. Customers will be.

Getting to know the competition

It is very easy to get bogged down in the detail of running your own business and not look up in order to see what is happening around you. However, you do need to follow closely what is going on in the marketplace – after all, you wouldn't set off for a walk with a blindfold on and expect to get very far!

Beware

Be prepared for new competitors especially if your products or services are highly successful.

Let's call the knowledge you have of your direct and indirect competitors your competitor intelligence. Like the favorite household pet, this needs regular feeding, grooming, petting, and general attention to grow big and strong.

Get out your magnifying glass

In order to build useful competitor intelligence, you should share the responsibility for information gathering around the company. This way, you will be able to pick up some of the more difficult information to find.

You will have to find time to tell people why this information is so important and what you will do with it. Make sure they

...cont'd

understand how each nugget helps you build a picture of the competitor and this will contribute to making your organization more successful.

Easy information

Encourage people to text or leave phone messages, create a special card or section in weekly reports, ask that each group meeting ends with a quick summary of competitive activity.

You should certainly introduce some kind of incentive and recognition for those who contribute.

Look at the size and structure of their organization

1. Check out any history of acquisitions.
2. Study their brand image and corporate reputations.
3. How would you sum up their business philosophy?
4. What evidence do you have to support this?
5. Write a list of product or service differences between you and your competitors.
6. Try to articulate what it is you believe their customers value about them.
7. Understand who, if not you, is the leader in the market and why.
8. Don't forget to look at their staff, how they conduct themselves and their dress code.
9. You might also be able to get a handle on their staff turnover (it's never a good sign if employees have left before their business cards are even printed).

Keep your eyes and ears open

Also use websites, literature, customer feedback, newspaper or trade magazine cuttings, products, trade shows, and customers to build a picture of your competitors and what they're up to. Keep a note of sales promotions and unusual sales activity. Like your pet though, don't forget how important it is to tend this file – don't just collect loads of stuff and bung it in a drawer.

Don't forget

Keep a scrapbook of useful bits and bobs but don't forget how important it is to tend this file to make it really useful

Look for the Achilles heel

Identify any chinks in their armor. Where is their organization weak? Then use this analysis to see where you should be stronger. You will also find it easier to identify areas of the market that you can take a leadership position in.

Answer these 6 VIP questions...

1. What makes your competitor(s) great?
2. What are their products like (features and benefits) and how do they compare with yours?
3. How good are their employees (managers, marketers, sales, product development, customer services, etc)?
4. Where do they sell their product/services?
5. Who are their biggest customers?
6. What has your competitor got that you haven't?

Try involving anyone who is familiar with them—customers, distributors, suppliers, your sales reps and customer services—in your research.

...cont'd

Looking forward

You must know your competitors well so that you can pre-empt any threats and have contingency plans in place. The better you understand where your competitors have come from and what they are doing, the more likely you are to be able to predict where they are going (and therefore where you need to be paying particular attention).

Always collect evidence to support what you are being told – ensure your competitor intelligence is robust. You'll run into trouble if you base your strategy on rumor and gossip!

Don't forget your own Achilles heel!

Sometimes we can spend too long looking critically at the performance of our competitors and forget how we're doing! As hard as you're searching for their weaknesses, someone is scrutinizing you.

Try to think like your competitors and see the world through their eyes. For instance, where are you most vulnerable? A little navel gazing may just give you the edge when it comes to protecting your business growth...

Make a list of black spots where you believe yourself to be weak in your performance. Identify which competitor is strong in each of these areas. Understand what it is that they do so well and make that your benchmark.

2 A snapshot in time

We find that marketing works the way the grass grows. You can never see it, but every week you have to mow the lawn.

Andy Travis

A snapshot in time

Before you can set your strategy in stone, you'll need to complete a full situation analysis. Your situation analysis is a snapshot of what the world looks like now given your context. This basically means you being able to provide the rationale for your marketing objectives, plans and strategies.

Hot tip

Use these easy steps to analyse new business ideas.

Essential ingredients

In your situation analysis you should touch on –

1. The macro environment.
2. The market situation.
3. The competitive situation.
4. A customer analysis.
5. A product analysis.
6. A distribution analysis.
7. How your sales projection may change over time.

Don't do this alone – involve as many interested parties as you can. After all, they will probably be able to give you different perspectives and information. At least one positive outcome will be that you will increase the market awareness of your organization!

Marketing research

Marketing research exists to make your marketing more successful. However, this doesn't mean that you need to research everything before any decisions can be made – in fact, there are probably many instances when research would contribute very little to your plan. Good thinking time about a problem may be all that is needed to find your solution.

However, if you want to know what your customers think or feel about your product or service, you probably are going to have to ask them, using some form of market research. Be wary about taking shortcuts and asking other people what they think the customer wants – answers may well be loaded with bias and take you in the wrong direction.

Don't forget

You want facts not opinions.

Your market research output is meant to give facts not opinion, so you're best starting with facts and not opinion! Otherwise you're in danger of falling foul of rubbish in, rubbish out…

Where to start?

Once you know what you know, list what you need to find out. Be specific. This might include areas that will give you customer insight, competitor intelligence, market analysis, brand tracking and analysis.

Then write down where you're going to get the information from. List your sources of information and highlight areas where you're unsure about where to find answers.

Budget first

Allocate budget – this might limit the kind of research you can carry out! Market research is like a piece of string in regards to how much it can cost, so it's crucial to start with a budget in mind.

You have to use your judgment as to how much money you are prepared to invest in marketing research based on the value to you of the answers. Think about the end point and estimate how crucial this piece of jigsaw is to you.

How long?

Specify timeframe. Again, this will help you to decide what kind of research you can realistically complete in the time you have at your disposal.

Be realistic about what you can achieve – if you put aggressive timelines against the project, you have to be prepared to pay for it. You'll either be giving an agency a large sum of money or you and your team will be working 24/7 – is this the best use of your resources? Equally, if you don't have the information to take the project forward and this causes delays throughout the organization, you'd better have good reason for not allocating enough budget!

What type of research do I need?

Primary Research is gathered based on interaction with other people. It includes interviews, focus groups, one-to-one meetings, mystery shopping, surveys, and observation. You can spend a great deal of money here!

Secondary Research is usually much easier to collect than primary because it is based on written material, literature, broadcast media, reports, and studies. Trade associations, libraries, websites, company accounts, and professional institutes are all sources of secondary research material.

Which is best?

Primary research data is driven by you to get an answer to a specific question. It is therefore extremely pertinent to your business. The output will belong to you to use as you see fit.

Secondary data however, already exists and you are trying to build an answer out of the information you can find. Essentially, the data is already in the public domain and may have been used by other companies, including your competitors!

Finding new markets

The marketing process for exploring new geographical opportunities will look very familiar.

1. Complete a market feasibility study.
2. Write your market analysis.
3. Understand what you need to enter the market.
4. Develop your international marketing strategy.
5. Implement locally.
6. Develop a local web site.

Some generalizations

In China, relationship building is a main priority. So it is quite common to eat and drink together as a way of strengthening ties. Alcohol will be offered as a gesture of hospitality, so if you want to refuse it, be gracious!

Also, try not to use too many hand gestures when you're talking to your Chinese counterparts – your flapping hands will irritate as they distract their attention away from what you're saying.

The Japanese are more formal in business relationships than the Chinese. Take care not to sound rude by being too blunt. It's also easy to fall into the trap of believing your Japanese counterpart is holding back information or being secretive – it is more probable that he or she is just less demonstrative.

Russian business meetings still tend to be very formal. Your appearance is important so always dress in traditional business attire. Take a gift of food that can be shared at the meeting as socializing is highly valued as part of business conduct.

In the United States, managers and their employees often socialize as equals. There tend to be few closed doors in offices, people are on first name terms and all levels in the business hierarchy are very approachable. A short, firm handshake is a common form of greeting and there is plenty of eye contact and smiling (in contrast, if you were in some parts of Africa, a long, limp handshake would be more acceptable!).

In Germany, however, office doors tend to be closed and business meetings uninterrupted. There will be a clear agenda and meetings will run to time. Your German counterpart will pay attention to detail and be very methodical. So don't spend too much time chewing the fat – work time is productive time.

Your French colleague, on the other hand, is likely to be well dressed, charming, maybe a little flirtatious and prepared to give you plenty of time. If you're not careful, you will leave a lively and interactive meeting wondering what has actually been agreed!

In Britain, we work longer hours than our European colleagues. As a result, we tend to make time in meetings for breaks from the agenda, take short walks around the offices during the day yet sadly eat lunch at our desks! Punctuality is very important and it is seen as disrespectful to be late or to keep people waiting (this is common in all places where time is short).

In the Middle East, women should generally cover their heads and be escorted by a man to business meetings. It is commonly understood that showing the soles of your shoes, crossing your legs or using your left hand in social settings are also taboo.

Other examples of social no-no's include making the A-OK sign in Brazil, patting someone on the head in Thailand or kissing a member of the opposite sex in public in India.

Don't forget

These are generalisations and attitudes change over time.

How to be a cross-cultural whiz!

Hot tip

Budget allowing, spend some time visiting the countries where your customers are based.

1. Make time to understand the cultures you will be working with. Ask colleagues for their impressions and tips. Read up as much as you can before you meet.

2. Try to suspend any judgments you may have. It's important that you try to be receptive to each individual you meet without holding pre-conceptions.

3. Pay attention to the details of communication, including body language, behavior and words used. Watch social and business interaction and work out what makes people feel comfortable.

4. It can be very unfortunate if an inability to communicate successfully causes a problem. Avoid blaming any individual. Start from the premise that everyone is doing their best. Spend your energy on putting the problem right.

5. As you gain expertise and knowledge of cultural awareness, share your experiences and discoveries with your colleagues. Who knows, you may save them embarrassment by preventing a faux pas of their own!

6. First and foremost, keep your business objective at the forefront of whatever you do. Nothing focuses and builds teams, irrespective of cultures and backgrounds, like working to the same goal.

7. Relax! You're better at this than you think. The more you enjoy yourself, the easier you will be to work with!

Tips for success

Look at the size and structure of the organization –

1. Go and find out for yourself how different things are!
2. Identify people there who can give you local guidance.
3. Understand the market in general and specifically the market for your product.
4. Get legal advice to protect your intellectual property.
5. Build local relationships.
6. Accept that one marketing message is not necessarily going to apply to one large market (look at Europe for example). You are going to have to target your marketing activity very carefully.

"Understand the differences; act on the commonalities."

– Andrew Masondo, African National Congress.

Save the red faces!

Generally it is best to avoid jargon and slang in any communication, spoken or written. Really pay attention to this – every company develops its own shorthand as its culture develops. Anyone not familiar with your shorthand will be completely lost in minutes!

Sporting or war metaphors can be risky too. It's very easy to slip into pseudo military speak when talking about business issues, particularly whenever the word 'strategy' is mentioned.

Be careful. Your audience may not appreciate this (I remember a German colleague voicing his unease about the language being used in a Six Sigma business conference in the US).

Always start any project or communication from the point of view of the audience or interested parties. Even well thought through communications plans can go horribly wrong if the abilities or preferences of the audience aren't first taken into account – there's no point covering notice boards with well constructed announcements if no-one can read them!

When inviting people from different cultures to an event you are hosting, try to be sensitive to their social norms. There was almost a riot when colleagues from all over Europe were invited to a huge conference in the US and were then asked not to make physical contact when dancing in the evening!

The more the merrier

Remember to involve plenty of people – after all, if you're auditing marketing, there are many functions (sales, customer service, manufacturing, accounting, technical service, credit control, corporate communications, legal dept, to name but a few) with opinions that should be included.

Don't forget to include all the marketers as well! They are not necessarily responsible for existing processes for instance but will be expected to work within them. Without a doubt, they will have suggestions for improvements that can be made.

Marketing audit

Facing the truth!

If you want to know how effective your current marketing really is (and you do) you should conduct an audit.

Usually the audit reviews

1. Your existing marketing processes.
2. Your department's relationships with other functions.
3. The level of support and understanding given to marketing initiatives.
4. How well information is used.
5. How effective your marketing activity is.

You don't have to spend a fortune on this (although of course, you can). It is perfectly acceptable to write a list of the questions to which you want answers and start asking them!

Just ensure that you are consistent in the questions that you ask and in the way that you collect the answers. The feedback will be easier to collate and more meaningful.

Just a thought...

Why not do this as part of your situation analysis? It's a good discipline to check where you are on a regular basis and the output will help you shape your marketing plan...

Hot tip

You should do this exercise regularly – at least once a year.

Summary

- Complete a full situation analysis
- Identify what you know and what you have still to find out
- Set a market research budget
- Agree a timeline
- Audit your marketing capability

"Again, your challenge is not just to improve. It is to break the service paradigm in your industry or market so that customers aren't just satisfied, they're so shocked that they tell strangers on the street how good you are."

Jack Welch

3 The marketer's toolbox

You must have mindshare

before you can have marketshare.

Christopher M.Knight

V

The marketer's toolbox

As a marketer, you are responsible for collecting, sifting and condensing masses of information. The sheer size and complexity of the task can be overwhelming.

Don't attempt to reinvent the wheel when you start your marketing planning process! There are already great frameworks that are commonly used and much loved by marketers. They will provide structure for your analysis.

Adapt them to your particular circumstances (sometimes just changing the language can help) and use them as a starting point for collecting more detailed information.

By the way, many of them are presented as a matrix, so while you're gathering your thoughts at the front of the room, at least you can look purposeful as you draw the framework!

Hot tip 

Use the PEST worksheet on page 170

PEST Analysis

This is a tried and tested tool for presenting information about the macro environment you're reviewing. It's a way of capturing details of the factors you have to consider in your planning work.

1. At the top of the page (or whiteboard) start with a clear definition of the market.

2. Then either draw another matrix or write your headings on the left of the page.

Political (political stability, future legislation, trade regulations, employment laws, consumer protection, competition regulation).

Economic (growth, interest rates, taxation, exchange rates, inflation, unemployment, customer drivers).

Socio-demographic (population, age distribution, social mobility, lifestyle changes, living conditions, education, health, ethical issues, language).

Technological (research and development, government research spending, internet, mobile communications, rate of technology transfer, manufacturing maturity).

3. Finally, fill in the blanks! This is very good to use in combination with Porter's 5 Forces Analysis (coming next!). It can also be a good lead into your SWOT analysis (see page 38), particularly in brainstorming or workshop sessions.

Porter's 5 Forces Analysis

Do this exercise regularly - at least once a year, or if there are changes in PEST.

Michael E. Porter published "Competitive Strategy: Techniques for Analyzing Industries and Competitors" in 1980. You might not want to read the book, but will nevertheless be able to make very good use of this model!

This analysis is extremely useful when you're assessing a new market for attractiveness and profitability or wanting to look at the market situation you currently face.

It is also strategically important because you can use the results to maximize your advantages and identify potential pitfalls.

The forces

There are 5 forces, which influence what happens in every industry and every market –

Hot tip

Use Porters 5 Forces worksheet on P171

1. Existing competitors.
2. The threat of potential new competitors.
3. Substitutes for products offered.
4. The power of suppliers.
5. The power of customers.

Your challenge is to identify the forces at work in your market and come up with a strategic response to protect or grow your business. Easier said than done!

A. Force One – Existing Competitors

Generally, competitive rivalry will be high if –

- There is little product differentiation between competitors.
- If competitors are similar sizes.
- If there are low market growth rates.
- If it is expensive to exit the market.
- If the strategies of the competitors appear to be the same.

...cont'd

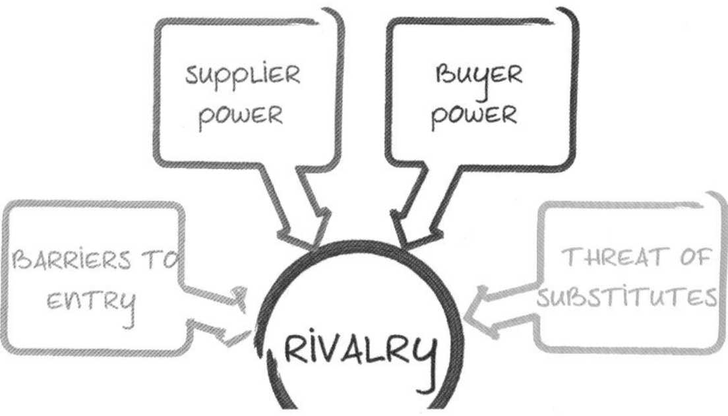

Strategic responses for your consideration –

- Don't compete on price.
- Look to other markets for growth.
- Avoid overcapacity.
- Differentiate your products.
- Buy a competitor!

B. Force Two – New Competitors

These will assess the market to see how easy it is to enter.

Tell-tale signs are –

- Low customer loyalty.
- Low investment costs and achievable manufacturing volumes.
- Easy access to suppliers.
- Few legislative barriers.

Strategic responses for your consideration –

- Strengthen your brand.
- Work closely with distribution and/or suppliers.
- Take cost out of your operation so that you can be more competitive.
- Protect your intellectual property with patents etc.

...cont'd

C. Force Three – Substitutes

Alternative products to those currently offered are a threat if the substitute is –

- Easy to switch to.
- If the price of the substitute falls.
- If customers are willing to change.

Strategic responses for your consideration –

- Emphasize (real or perceived) differences.
- Make it more costly to switch.
- Find out what your customers prefer.
- Enter the substitute market yourself!

D. Force Four – Suppliers

The suppliers of raw materials have varying degrees of power in a marketplace, depending on –

- The cost associated with switching suppliers.
- The number of suppliers available.
- If there is no substitute for the raw material.

Strategic responses for your consideration –

- Invest in supply chain management (see later chapter!) and training.
- Develop partnerships with suppliers.
- Explore ways of increasing their dependency on you.
- Take over a supplier!

E. Force Five – Customer or Buyer Power

This can be best seen in markets where –

- The product is not strategically important to the customer.
- They buy in bulk.
- Switching products is cheap.
- They are very price sensitive.
- Substitutes are readily available.

Strategic responses for your consideration –

- Increase loyalty.
- Introduce incentives.
- Deal direct rather than through distributors.
- Avoid purchase decisions based on price!

The SWOT

It takes one to know one!

Hot tip

Use the SWOT worksheet on P172

This is a simple matrix on which you will capture the...

1. Strengths
2. Weaknesses
3. Opportunities
4. Threats

that apply to your business in relation to competition.

Strengths and weaknesses refer to your product or service (internal issues), opportunities and threats to the external marketplace.

Your SWOT is best completed with the help of as many people from different functions (sales, marketing, customer service, product development, management, even customers) as you can involve – a variety of perspectives are invaluable.

It doesn't take long to complete (about 15 minutes if you're all focused!) and is a great way to kick-off a planning meeting.

Just remember that this is a very subjective tool. Be specific in your observations and keep comments short and simple.

As I said earlier (and great suggestions are worth repeating!) it's a good idea to use this in combination with a completed PEST and 5 Forces analysis as these provide the context for your SWOT.

cont'd

Don't forget 

Some of these are opinions and not facts.

Summary

1. Complete a PEST analysis of the macro environment (the market) in order to review the situation you are in. It has four key perspectives -

   POLITICAL

   ECONOMIC

   SOCIAL

   TECHNOLOGICAL

2. Then a 5 Forces Analysis in order to assess and analyze your competitive strength and position in the market. Porter suggests that the five forces that drive competition are-

   Existing competitive rivalry between suppliers

   Threat of new market entrants

   Bargaining power of buyers

   Power of suppliers

   Threat of substitute products

3. Followed by a SWOT (for your business proposition or idea), which provides a simple framework for gathering and reviewing data about strategy, business direction, products and so on.

   Strengths and Weaknesses capture internal factors (performance, quality, price, people, skills etc)

   Opportunities and Threats refer to external factors (markets, trends, competition, economics, politics etc)

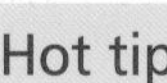

Hot tip

Try applying the SWOT model to different situations from acquisition or a potential business partnership to personal career planning or relationships!

Follow me... I have a plan!

Next to doing the right thing, the most important thing is to let people know you are doing the right thing

John D. Rockefeller

Follow me... I have a plan!

Beware

Your targets must be as realistic as possible. Unrealistic targets will de-motivate your staff and cost you your credibility.

A marketing strategy is a declaration of where you are heading and broadly how you will get there. You may also wish to include a timeframe. For example, "to be the largest supplier of recyclable cell phones in Europe by 2012" or "to be the brand of first choice in UK consumer health markets" or "to increase market share by ten points by making new products available through emerging channels".

Use "what if" thinking to explore strategic options and come up with new ideas.

Look at your business strategies from a different perspective. Rather than an employee, adopt the viewpoint of a competitor or customer.

Your strategy needs to be memorable and credible so do test it out on colleagues. If there are derisory guffaws around the room, the chances are that you've misread the situation (resources, competition, customer behavior). Your strategy must be realistic if it's to stand the test of time.

Pass it on

Your strategy must not be a secret from your team and should be around for years rather than months. You need the strategy to be influencing business priorities throughout the company.

Let it grow, let it grow!

Your number one challenge is likely to be how to get bigger. There isn't a marketing manager alive who hasn't wrestled with this one. Fortunately, some of the groundwork has been done for you.

The Ansoff's Matrix

Ansoff's Product/Market Matrix

First published in The Harvard Review in 1957, this matrix captures strategies for growth. Basically, it suggests that you have four options for growth –

Use the Ansoff's Product/Market Matrix worksheet on P173

MARKET \ PRODUCT	PRESENT	NEW
PRESENT	MARKET PENETRATION	PRODUCT DEVELOPMENT
NEW	MARKET DEVELOPMENT	DIVERSIFICATION

1. Sell more of your existing products to existing customers (market penetration).

   Why not consider –

   - Introducing loyalty schemes to increase usage.
   - Running aggressive promotional campaigns in parallel with keen pricing to discourage new competitors.
   - Using your marketing communications and pricing strategies to maintain or increase market share.

2. Sell your existing products to new customers/markets (market development).

   Why not consider ways to –

   - Access new geographical markets.
   - Use new distribution channels and design pricing structures, which open up new customers or markets.

3 Take new products to existing customers (product development).

Why not consider –

Investing in the skills and competencies needed in order to develop new or modified products (see Chapter 5, King Pee - Products and Services).

4 Find new markets for new products (diversification).

Take a deep breath before you consider this one –

Many people would consider this to be the most risky (and expensive) of the four growth strategies as your aim is to move into unfamiliar markets with new products.

You'll inevitably hear people talking about this. Don't panic. It's simple to understand and use. It will of course, be harder to achieve!

Gap analysis

Basically, identify where you are now (base line), where you want to be in the future (usually somewhere better than where you are now) and there's your gap!

The challenge, of course, is how you fill it with marketing activity that closes the gap.

I have a plan

People should want to read the marketing plan – it provides the framework for your marketing activities.

Your plan must state your goals (mission); what you intend to achieve over the next 12 months (objectives); what you will need to achieve these objectives (strategies); and which parts of the marketing mix you intend to use (tactics) with a plan, timescale and events.

Take your time

As a general rule, the marketing plan will take longer to complete the larger your company. Basically, this is because you will have to involve more people to ensure the plan is robust.

Allow enough time to co-ordinate input, analyze material and create the output – a late plan means that people are working for a period of time without direction. Preparation time must be built into your calendar – and into the diaries of those you want to involve!

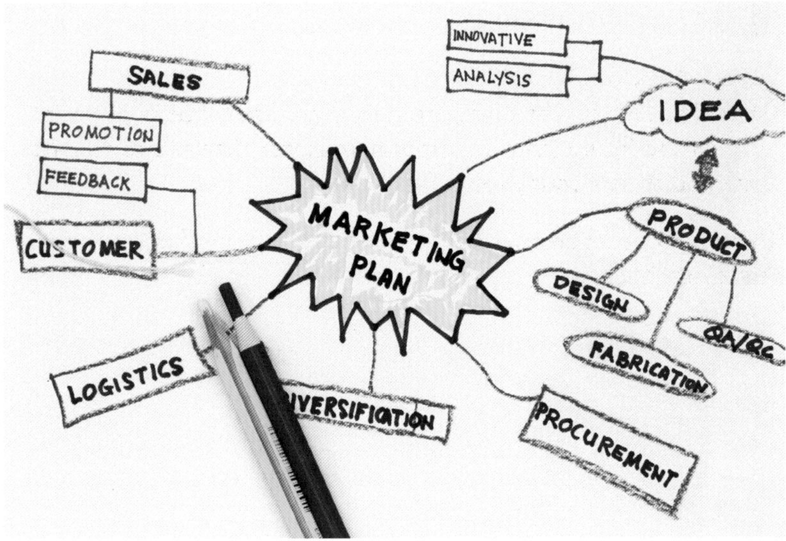

Beware

Creating a complex planning process, which takes a year to complete and allows you no time for implementation!

...cont'd

Hot tip

Make your marketing plan comprehensive but clear and concise. No-one likes to read lengthy reports.

Start with the end in mind!

The marketing plan must be easy to read and accessible.

Before writing anything, take your time to think about what the finished product should look like, who will use it, and how it will be communicated. Ask colleagues what they would like to see in terms of presentation.

See if you can condense the main points onto a small card, which can easily be carried by employees so that everyone is clear about the direction for the next twelve months.

Make a list of what you already know and what information you need. Work out who or where you need information from in order to understand the situation fully. Be sure to collect as many perspectives as possible and as much factual information as you can (beware the highly opinionated who have no evidence to support their views!).

Your plan should include –

1. Executive summary.
2. Industry analysis.
3. Description of your target market.
4. Description of your competitors.
5. Marketing strategy.
6. Details of your product or service.
7. Forecasts and financial analysis.
8. Marketing budget (including advertising and promotional plans).
9. Pricing strategy.

Paperwork, paperwork

Beware the marketing planning process that just becomes a bureaucratic nightmare! We've all seen this – the target becomes the timely completion of the forms rather than providing high quality information. Maddeningly, this rigidity also prevents you adapting the plan should the market conditions alter during the year. Yet we're all agreed that if the plan doesn't remain relevant, it will soon lose importance to your team and inevitably fail.

Hot tip

Review and adjust your marketing plan regularly to reflect changes in the market place.

It is a good idea to periodically tweak the previous year's input rather than start each year with a blank piece of paper. At least this way, marketers are looking to identify changes in their markets.

A best kept secret

Another possible reason for your marketing plan to fail is lack of buy-in!

Avoid this by –

1. ensuring that you have senior management approval.
2. checking that action plans across functions use the marketing plan as a basis for goal setting.
3. insisting that the marketing team champion the strategy and plan.
4. making sure that any sales bonus/incentives are a reflection of the objectives.

Let me tell you a story...

Hot tip

Keep your own team involved during the process to get their commitment

So, once you've written the plan and had it approved, communicate it! Schedule presentation times in your diary and target every group in your organization.

You need to make sure that your colleagues are familiar with the plan to the point that they can understand how they are involved in the company reaching its goals.

Pay attention to sales, customer services, manufacturing, and finance – each function is essential to your marketing success. Allow time in your communications plan to spend time with each of the functions.

Leave a user-friendly summary for each person to keep in their diary. Make the communication of the marketing plan an event and time it so that each function can incorporate relevant objectives into their own function targets and incentives.

You should also communicate your plan to key customers and distributors. They need to know about new products in the pipeline, planned promotional activity and target markets in order to incorporate this into their own plans. So be prepared to answer questions – they may well expect you to be able to give detail about when you will provide training, relevant materials and inventory.

What gets measured gets managed

Set in place metrics that you can use to tell whether your plan is on track. You need to collect feedback in order to discover where things are going wrong, ideally before you miss financial goals.

Put in place market metrics that can tell you how well you as a business are able to respond to customer enquiries and problems; how many product trials are initiated and levels of repeat purchases; the level of support you receive from distributors in terms of market coverage, inventory levels, and take up of new products.

Acid test!

Once your plan is written, you should be able to see that all your marketing activities cascade from your strategy. If you can't see any connection, something is wrong with either your strategy or your management of marketing resources!

The 4Ps (or marketing mix)

The vast majority of all your marketing management decisions will fall into the following four areas –

Product: is your offering clearly defined, both features and benefits, actual or needed? (See Chapter 6.)

Pricing: is your product or service priced at a level that is both acceptable to customers and still profitable? (See Chapter 7.)

Promotion: have you clear plans as to how you intend to communicate about your service or product? (See Chapter 8.)

Place: where will you sell your product or service and how will you get it there? (See Chapter 9.)

Use the 4Ps to prompt you to address all aspects of your product or service offering – you can use it at both strategic and tactical levels, for existing products or concepts. Again, use a simple matrix to present this in meetings or written reports.

Use the worksheet on p174.

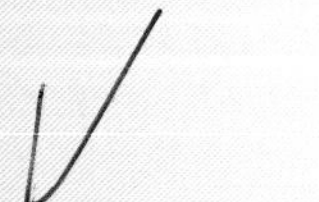

3 More Ps!

In order to flesh out your analysis, you can always add to the traditional 4Ps. The additional prompts (People, Process and Physical Presence) will remind you to pay attention to other critical areas of your business.

People

Well, we've all had contact at some point or other with an employee who has single-handedly destroyed any good impressions you may have had about the company they work for. Whether it is a surly shop assistant, a rude call centre contact or an offhand receptionist, you as the customer are left feeling disenchanted with your contact experience. Chances are you won't want to repeat the experience.

As a marketer, you are responsible for ensuring that your customer contact points are all well handled and that the customer-facing staff can understand the importance of their contribution to this.

We'll discuss this further in Chapter 10.

Process

It's really important that you understand all the processes that exist around getting the product to your customer and those that are about keeping the customer. This doesn't just mean sales processes but also how you manage complaints, delays, invoicing, and quality problems.

Physical Presence

Basically, what impression does your customer get when they first step into your reception area or meeting rooms? When they see your delivery vans scooting about in the streets are your customers impressed? You should even consider whether the appearance of your staff gives a fair representation of your company.

This isn't rocket science – try to be dispassionate, put yourself in your customer's shoes and use your eyes! Are your assets working for you? Do they reflect the way you want the company to be seen?

Project life cycle

1. Try using sheets of brown paper taped around the room on which to plot your customer contact processes.

2. Include everyone involved in the workflows in the workshop.

3. Ask each process 'owner' to draw every part of the process, however complicated.

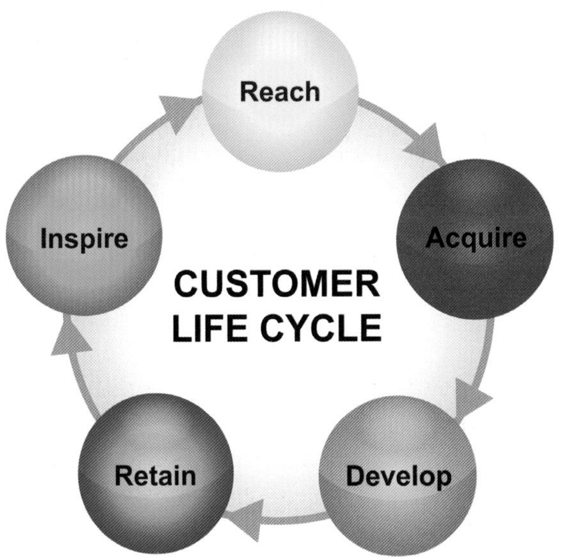

This will give you a clear illustration of how many processes you currently have, how complex they are or not and how many people are involved in delivering customer satisfaction.

You may also be able to immediately see opportunities for process improvement. Focus on areas of weakness (look for overlaps, processes that involve numerous employees/ departments, processes that don't deliver clear benefits) and make it a priority to make that process better, be it shorter, simpler, less costly.

We cover business processes in more detail in Chapter 10.

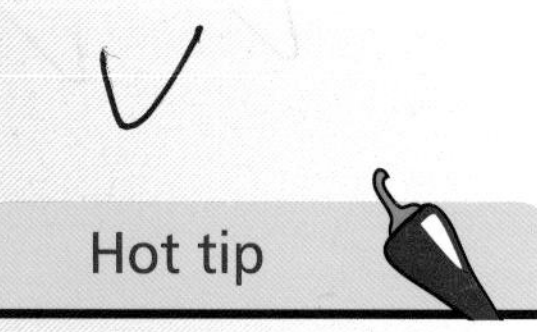

Summary

Hot tip

Keep your metrics SMART (specific, measurable, achievable, realistic and with a timescale).

1. Write your marketing strategy (and ensure you include many perspectives in its formulation!)

2. Review your marketing strategy with your whole team. Test it for credibility

3. Quantify your gap analysis. What exactly are you going to do to get to where you want to be?

4. Generate your marketing plan (and keep it logical and easy to follow!)

5. Communicate the agreed plan and metrics (why not produce pocket sized versions that can be easily distributed and referred to?)

King Pee (Products & Services)

A market is never saturated with a good product, but it is quickly saturated with a bad one.

Henry Ford

King Pee (Products & Services)

These are the lifeblood of your organization. Treat them with the respect they deserve!

You should love your products and services like a parent loves a child – you bring them, shiny and new, into the world and you tend them through both good and difficult times! Whatever happens, you do your best to help them reach their full potential, giving encouragement and gentle nudges in the right direction, should they veer off course…

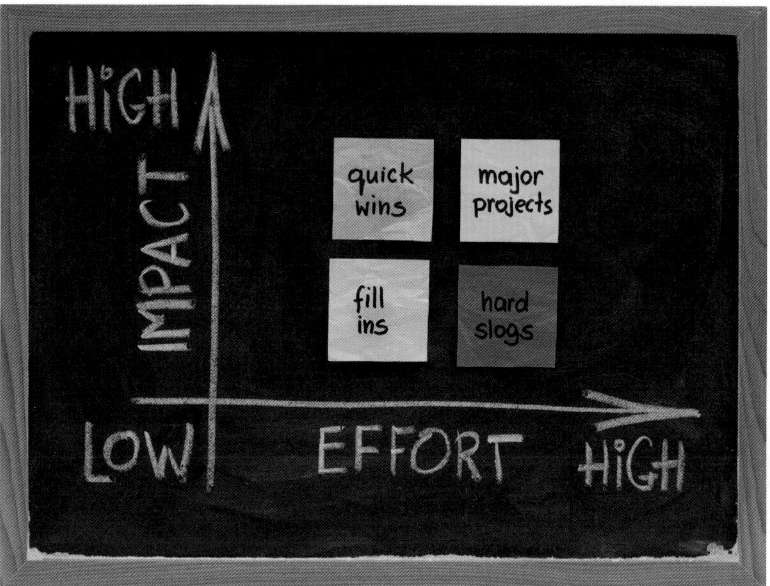

Product management

I think this role is worth a little definition!

Basically, a product manager is responsible for the health and success of the product(s). This breaks down into two clearly defined areas of product planning and product marketing.

 Product planning (inbound activity)

This involves you providing the product definition (you should include target market, product features, advantages and benefits, competitive analysis) and design (how the product will look). No pressure then! All you need is oodles of creativity, product and market knowledge, an understanding of manufacturing processes and customer requirements.

It's worth revisiting shelved projects every now and then to check that an idea once had hasn't now come into its own.

You may well be approached by private inventors who need your help to get the product to market. Make time to review their ideas but do check the legal issues such as patents and licensing agreements.

2 Product marketing (outbound activity)

You'll take responsibility for the management of the product through its life cycle (from launch right through to decline).

Bear in mind the product positioning in relation to the rest of the portfolio.

Make sure your customers know that you have a new product to sell and emphasize what makes it different

Never waste the opportunity to shout about an upgrade, however minor the tweaking may seem to you!

Remember to look at existing products for new markets – one man's meat is another man's poison and so on!

Don't forget

Try to look for new markets for existing products.

Product Life Cycle

Now, this marketing model is not a matrix! But it is INVALUABLE! Your product life cycle analysis will simplify your life.

Broadly speaking, there are four stages in the life of a product or service. When you have identified where your product is on the curve, understanding what is likely to happen and therefore what you should be planning for, becomes easier.

You'll inevitably hear people talking about this. Don't panic. It's simple to understand and use. It will of course, be harder to achieve!

Generally, product life cycles are getting shorter so you must proactively manage your product through its life cycle.

There are many things you can do to affect the life of your products and with careful tweaking, you can extend that life.

You should also aim to minimize the time withdrawing your products – once they fall into decline, you want them out of your portfolio so that you can concentrate resources on new and growing products.

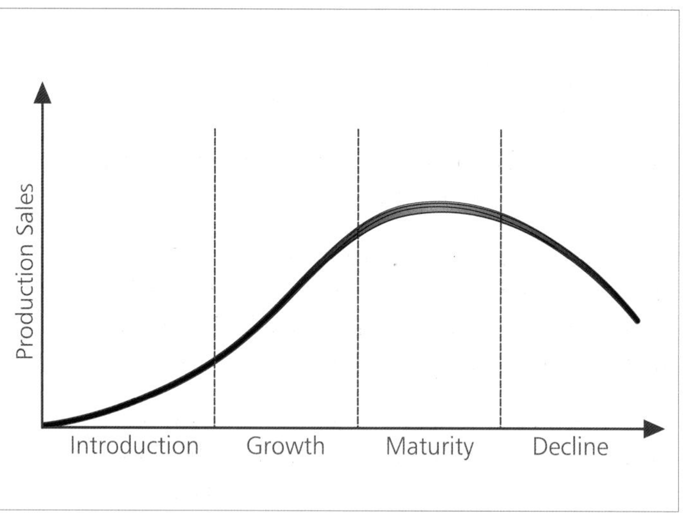

cont'd

The first phase is 'introduction'

At this time don't be surprised if new products need minor alterations to get absolutely right.

Identify a relatively small number of customers (early adopters) who will be excited enough to try out something new. These customers are invaluable – they will work with you while you sort out any problems and can provide excellent feedback.

Now your competitors are busy! Product quality is good, product features are being promoted and prices are coming down. Customers have LOTS of choice!

Concentrate your marketing communications effort on building awareness.

The next phase is 'growth'

At this point there is much more competitive activity (which means that product features are being promoted, prices are starting to fall and the customer has lots of choice) and overall quality of product is good.

As a marketer, you should be working hard to ensure that you are getting your share of this market – customer take-up is fast and you cannot afford to be left behind. This is not the time to have supply problems!

Watch your competitors closely – they'll be trying to make product better, faster and cheaper than you.

Make sure your distribution network is big enough so that customers have easy access to your products.

Now your market is moving into 'maturity'

Your sales are really made up of replacements and product extensions, so extend this phase with a gradual build up of product features – don't blow them all on one launch!

At this time it is important that you concentrate on having a strong brand and competitive pricing to ensure that existing customers stay with you (or add features which build on their earlier investment).

...cont'd

Finally, you are in the 'decline' of the market

Now you'll see major competitors leaving and overall product quality may begin to fall. Sales will start to drop as demand falls. Customers will inevitably start to look elsewhere for better alternatives.

New product development should be well underway in your company. Just be careful not to launch anything too quickly, thereby speeding up obsolescence of the old products… but don't sit on something new and exciting (and more profitable) in order to squeeze every last drop of revenue out of the old range!

Of course, this is just a model and ultimately you must learn to trust your creativity and judgment. Nevertheless, the product life cycle is an excellent starting point for exploring your options.

Boston Matrix

This is another well-used marketing tool, designed by the Boston Consulting Group to summarize product portfolio planning.

Use the Boston Matrix worksheet on P175.

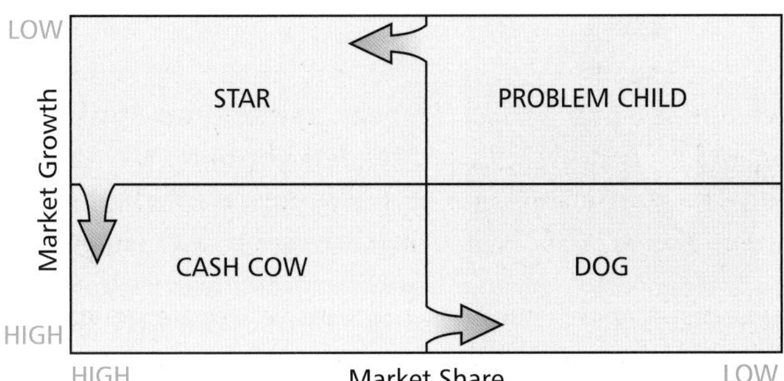

First of all, begin by plotting your products on the matrix. Then add those of your competitors. Ideally you want to have **stars** (products with growing sales and high market share) and **cash cows** (high market share, slow or no growth) and you want your competitors to have **dogs** (low market share and no growth)!

Problem children are expensive to keep (low market share in a fast growing market) but you are investing in them in the hope that they become stars in the future... the downside is that they may become dogs instead and you've got another product to lose from your portfolio!

This analysis might help you to identify which products you should support more with marketing communications or where you need to invest in more product development. It will also give you a fix on the health of your competitors' product ranges and may alert you to potential threats as they move their problem children into stars and withdraw dogs in favor of cash cows!

Product manager's responsibilities continue!

You'll also be responsible for all the external communications related to your product. This will include datasheets, brochures, websites, exhibitions, advertising and PR.

It's certainly easier to be a great product manager if you love your products!

Product forecasts

Don't forget

Forecasting is important for all aspects of business planning.

Forecasting is not always fun but is critical to the smooth running of your company. This is a time to put on your analytical hat and steer away from too much creativity!

You're going to use these forecasts (in value and units) to drive manufacturing, sales incentives, product launch plans and customer service among other things. You may also be using the forecast to justify marketing budgets.

Get the forecasts right and you're a hero.

Get them wrong and you could face supply or service problems (good news for your competitors) or huge overspends on your budgets (bad news for you and the company).

Don't feel you should produce the forecast alone – ask your sales people to provide you with their territory forecasts with some justification of how they've got to those numbers (bear in mind that they may want to keep estimates low in order to beat targets and win incentives!).

By regularly reviewing and adjusting forecasts you can reflect changes in sales patterns by product, be they seasonal adjustments, changes in your product mix, or as a result of promotional activity.

How to launch products

1. Position your product. Confirm target pricing.
2. Involve engineering, manufacturing, sales, marketing, customer services, and product support in your initial planning.
3. Write a launch plan, including contingency plans.
4. Communicate launch plan.
5. Allocate resources to support the launch (6 months minimum).
6. Set targets.
7. Get buy-in to targets!
8. Design and order packaging.
9. Complete all documentation (user manuals, etc).
10. Complete your marketing materials, advertising, product brochures, web pages, press releases.
11. Establish sales channels.
12. Product training for sales and customer services completed.
13. Build stock.
14. Train channels.
15. Update product forecasts.
16. Measure, measure, measure.
17. Share success stories and tweak plan.

Hot tip

Get your whole team involved in as many stages as possible.

✓

Tips for meaningful forecasts

1. Be very specific about what period your forecast is relevant to.

2. Collect input from sales (including distributors if possible) and sales management, and build in events or market conditions that may have an effect.

3. A twelve month rolling forecast (units and value) is best reviewed on a quarterly or even monthly basis by all functions (marketing, sales, manufacturing, customer service).

4. Always pay attention to a worst case forecast so you can rein in spending if necessary.

5. Remember to build in the time delay between taking the order and receiving payment if your business uses cash-based accounting.

6. Base your new product forecast on a test market. Use your experience in a small geographical area and extrapolate forwards.

7. Look at your sales history as a predictor for what is likely to happen going forward.

Product packaging

Your product packaging has two purposes:

1. To look good to attract customers.

2. To protect your product so that it's intact when it gets to its final destination.

Don't forget

You want your product to stand out but note the features of existing successful products.

You must pay attention to how you want your product to look on the shelves, in the catalogue, on the internet. Your product packaging will give the customer another impression of your company so it's worth getting it right. (See the later section in this chapter on Branding.)

Look around you

It's a good idea to check out how products similar to yours are packaged. Look in retailers and distributors. Make a note of what materials are used and the size and shape of the packaging. Look for information on the packaging, including color, branding, product information. See how well the packaging seems to cope with being transported.

Remember the customer

You should then think about how you can make your packaging work for you as a marketing and sales tool. Start with the customer in mind – what do you believe will appeal to them? What will draw them to your product over others? How can you prevent them screaming in frustration as they find yet another piece of bendy wire wrapped round their toddler's new doll on Christmas morning (that one is heartfelt!)?

Grab some attention

Then think how you can make your product stand out. For example, if the competition tends to be conservative in presentation, think about using bright colors on your packaging.

Do also make sure that your company logo is clearly visible –whichever way the product is arranged on a shelf.

A picture says a thousand words

Hot tip

Be aware of the latest political and popular trends.

Avoid overcrowding the packaging. Better to include a leaflet, or direct customers to your website.

Use pictures rather than words where you can – this is particularly useful if you intend to ship overseas.

Less is more

Make sure your product packaging is efficient in terms of size. No-one appreciates unnecessarily large or bulky packaging anymore – it's environmentally unfriendly, costly to ship and too labor intensive to keep shelves stocked.

Work on the functionality of the product packaging by making it easier to recycle, open or use for storage. Ask for ideas from people in the warehouse or distributors who handle packaged product to see what you can add to the design to make it more user-friendly.

Your product itself will probably dictate the packaging material you should use. Don't let your experimental side run away with you – remember that you need the packaging to protect your product until it is unwrapped and ready for use!

KISS (Keep It Simple Stupid)

Finally, keep your packaging simple and fit for purpose! Avoid over-packaging, over-decorating, over-selling… now is a time to consider sustainability and all things green.

What is a brand?

"Brand is a name, sign or symbol used to identify items or services of the sellers and to differentiate them from goods of competitors." The Dictionary of Business and Management.

"Simply put, a brand is a promise. By identifying and authenticating a product or service it delivers a pledge of satisfaction and quality." Walter Landor.

Great brands don't just happen. They are nurtured over time. Brand management is a key marketing activity. It will challenge your creativity!

Don't forget

Brands have to be nurtured.

The brand is your company's 'personality'

You can separate brand into brand image and brand values. The former is any graphics or colors you adopt, the latter is what emotional response your company generates with its customers.

You can obviously control your image by making sure there is consistency in the presentation of your company. Be aware of keeping your look the same across all your representations – ideally your logo, graphics, typeface, colors, etc are instantly recognizable to your customers.

Sadly, it is far less easy to control what people actually say or write about you!

Pay particular attention to your brand values (your personality and what you stand for) and how they are reflected throughout the company. Think about your corporate culture, communications, products, and services. Your brand values should guide decision making, be supported by all levels of management, and be seen in all customer contact points.

...cont'd

For instance –

- How well trained are your staff?
- What is your returns policy?
- How much authority do your customer services team have to sort out problems?
- What involvement does your company have in local events and fundraising?
- How green are your manufacturing processes?
- How fairly do you treat suppliers?
- And so it goes on!

Why do I want a brand?

With your brand, you give an implied promise that the quality of a product or service will be transferable across the existing range or future products.

So?

Having a strong brand will help you introduce new products quickly, give you a competitive advantage and improve your overall image.

It will also help you in times of economic uncertainty, for instance in a price war or recession.

Companies with strong brands tend to weather quality or supply issues better as customers trust the company to be working in their best interest.

Branding fever!

You may decide to add more complexity to your branding work by having both a corporate brand and then developing product brands!

Your product brand could fall into one of several categories

1. Premium (high price).

2. Fighting (developed to take on a competitive product).

3. Economy (where price is a deciding factor).

4. Individual (where each product in a company is given a separate name).

5. Family (one name for related products).

The branding process

1. Identify the words that describe your company/product and use them to create a brand statement.

2. Ask yourself what makes your offer special? What makes your company or product stand out? Are your brand words reflected in your product?

3. Conduct a brand perception survey (working with customers, employees, suppliers and prospects, distributors) which allows you to find out how your company or brand is perceived.

4. Review the feedback. Be objective and open to making changes.

5. Hold a brand workshop which will give you a chance to make sure everyone has the same understanding of brand and can then work together towards producing your positioning statement, a list of brand values, the brand promise and a brand story. It's also an opportunity to collect input on imagery, colors, taglines, etc.

6. Articulate your plan for managing (and measuring) your brand going forwards.

VIP brand workshop questions

What products or services do we offer? Define the qualities of these products or services.

- Focus on your product or service. This is the lifeblood of your business.
- Ensure it is well managed and resourced. Pay attention to the detail, including forecasts, launch plans, quality issues, communication plans.
- Use your product life cycle analysis (Introduction, Growth, Maturity and Decline of the product life cycle curve) and Boston Matrix (Star, Cash Cow, Dog and Problem Child) to guide marketing decisions.
- Invest in branding and packaging. Manage your "look" but also your promise....
- Will your brand ever be big enough to become a verb? "To Google" for instance or "to hoover"?

Hot tip

After the workshop create the profile of your brand based on the output; publish your results and ask for comment and finally document and circulate your brand strategy!

6 Queen Pee (Pricing)

Half the money I spend on marketing is wasted, and the problem is I do not know which half.

Lord Leverhulme

The bottom line!

Managing your Pricing Strategy

This has got to be one of the greatest challenges you face in marketing! After all, you don't want to price your product too high and have customers look for an alternative. Nor can you afford to set prices too low and see your profits disappear.

Market based pricing takes into account the current situation in the market with regard to your competitors, customers and competitive position. Your aim is to balance product attractiveness with customer value.

Cost based pricing begins with your actual costs to make the product and your desired profit margin. This tends to be used in markets where there is little product differentiation (for example, commodity markets, like oil or gas).

Just be sure that you really know the actual costs of the product or service before setting the price! This might be the perfect time to make good friends with your company bean counter or accountant – you absolutely do not want to base your pricing strategy on inaccurate numbers!

It is important that you determine your pricing strategy before you start product development. Otherwise, how will you know what to design?

So, before setting your prices...

You have a number of things to consider that will affect the final price points!

1. Your brand value (recognized brands can get higher prices).
2. Your competitors' pricing (and are your target customers aware of it?).
3. The prices of your existing products.
4. The quality of your product (customers will pay more for high quality).
5. Customer expectations (what they think is a reasonable price).
6. Your volume goals.
7. Your manufacturing costs.
8. How your competitors will react to your pricing strategy!

New product pricing – which way to go?

Don't forget

Don't forget that manufacturers can only recommend a list price.

When you're introducing a new product to the market, you do have an overwhelming number of options regarding price. You should consider the level to set your prices based on your plans for the product (or your strategy), so have a look at the following list to see if there's one that suits!

Premium pricing is ideal when your product is unique (high quality, high price) and you have substantial competitive advantage.

Penetration pricing means that you hold prices artificially low in order to build volume. Once you have reached your target turnover, you can start raising prices.

Economy pricing is appropriate when you are committed to providing a low priced product, such as own label.

Skimming is when you know you can charge high prices to a quality-sensitive market until competitive activity brings the prices down. Remember the product life cycle? This strategy is often aimed at Early Adopters (people who will pay more to be the first to own new technology, etc).

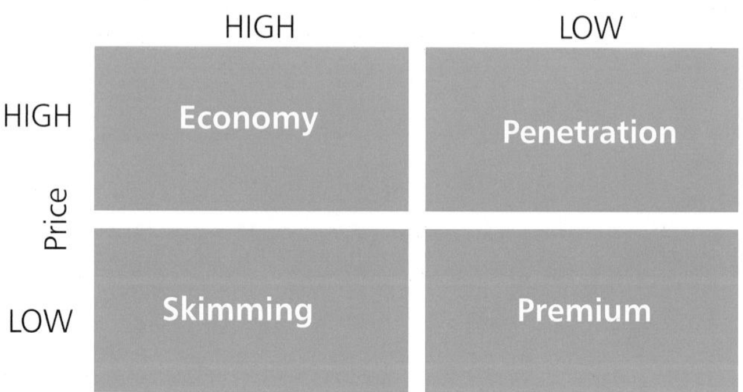

Pricing Strategies Matrix

You may well have to build a discount structure into your calculations. Distributors, wholesalers, retailers, and agents will all be expecting a varying percentage of the product price.

Advanced pricing strategies!

Psychological pricing or odd-even pricing is when you use a price that ends with the number 9. Price sensitive customers often perceive rounded up prices as significantly higher.

Just be careful that you don't do more harm than good by making your product seem cheap if the customer also thinks it is of poorer quality.

Product line pricing or price lining – you may want to slip a new product into an existing product line and so will base your pricing on a number that 'fits'.

Optional product pricing – here you can start adding optional extras once the customer has started buying. Airlines often take this approach – on top of your ticket price, the customer can opt to pay for priority check-in, meals, reserved seating, etc.

Captive product pricing – once the customer has bought a certain product at a low price, accessories or replacement parts have to be bought at a high price. Examples of this can be seen with electric toothbrushes and replacement heads, razors and blades, etc.

Geographical product pricing is often seen in the car market, where left hand versus right hand drive can affect product pricing in different countries across the world.

Promotional pricing is one of the most commonly used pricing strategies (buy 3 for 2, % off list price, etc) because it allows you to experiment with price points to see what customers respond to best.

However, just be careful that you're not discounting products and giving away profit for no good reason. Discounts to retailers won't necessarily get passed on to the consumer – as a result, they increase their profits and you don't see any uplift in sales!

Also remember that constantly drawing the customer's attention to price can make them less brand loyal and more likely to shop around for cheaper product!

Perceived value pricing – perhaps difficult to give a value to, your product, service and brand may nevertheless have a perceived value to the customer. You've got to be very confident that you're reading your market accurately.

...cont'd

Competitive pricing is particularly applicable if you're coming into an established market and want to give the market leader a run for their money! You match the product in terms of quality and availability but offer it to the customer at lower prices. This should mean that you are offering much better value than your competitor.

Don't expect your competitors to sit back and watch you mop up their customers! If they are bigger, more aggressive or financially stronger, they may well try to beat you at your own game and introduce their own price reductions.

Product bundling strategy basically means that the more the customer buys from you, the greater their discount. Cable companies use this with their pricing structures for television, broadband and telephone line rental.

No matter what business you're in, your customers all want the same three things: They want it for free, they want it perfect, and they want it now.

Rob Rodin, CEO of Marshall Industries

Top tips for pricing

The further along the life cycle, the lower your prices need to be!

1 Generally, low volume sales in a growing market allows you to charge higher prices (as long as there is market demand) and high volume sales tend to result in lower profit margins but high turnover.

2 It's also much easier to bring prices down than increase them if you've got it wrong!

3 Try unbundling products as they age – that way you can drop prices but not reduce profit.

4 You need to be making profit in order to have a successful business, so pay attention to costs.

5 If you want to continue to offer good value you should pay attention to changing market conditions and price accordingly. Review your pricing structure regularly.

6 It is worth understanding your competitors' pricing structure but beware just trying to fit your prices alongside… they may have got it wrong!

7 Test price sensitivity in small geographical areas before rolling out nationally in order to get a handle on the likely customer response.

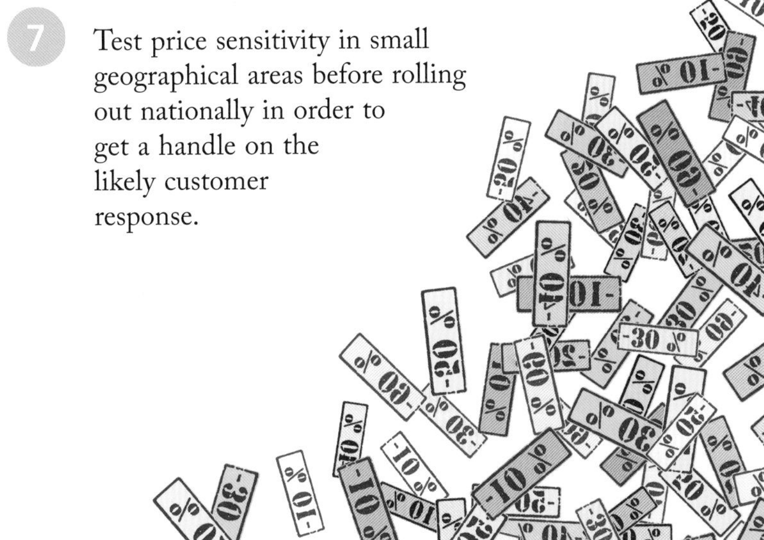

Don't forget

The bottom line!

Red alert!

1. Review your own and competitor pricing….market based or cost based pricing

2. Explore your strategic pricing options (Premium, Penetration, Economy or Skimming)

3. Understand the **actual** costs of your product or service

4. Estimate the perceived value of your product, service or brand

5. Set pricing….remember, it's always harder to increase prices than to lower them once your product or service is launched!

7 Prince Pee (Promotion)

I once used the word "obsolete" in a headline, only to discover that 43% of housewives had no idea what it meant. In another headline I used the word "ineffable," only to discover that I didn't know what it meant myself.

David Ogilvy

Prince Pee (Promotion)

Before you decide how to communicate (advertising, selling, sales promotion, public relations, etc) be clear about your objectives. Do you want to generate new customers, increase usage by existing customers, encourage existing customers to buy related products, or reward current customers? Having made this strategic choice, you will find it easier to decide on the most appropriate way to reach your target audience.

Advertising

Whichever medium you choose (print, TV or radio), one of the main reasons that you're advertising is in order to increase sales.

1. Get a good baseline in place – which means you have to understand what you achieve without advertising activity.

2. Then monitor your sales carefully during and after your campaign. If you're running different kinds of campaigns at the same time, ensure you understand exactly where your responses and conversions are coming from.

3. Then offset your cost of advertising against increased sales revenue in order to measure which activity is most effective.

It's said that companies that reduce advertising activity when times are hard take far longer to recover than those which continue to invest, thereby protecting their business.

Who, What, When, Where, How?

Remember to start your campaign planning with the answers to the following:

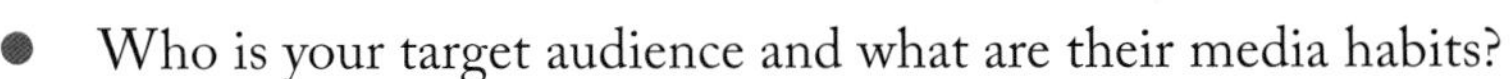

- Who is your target audience and what are their media habits?
- You need to know what television programmes, radio stations and newspapers your target audience prefer.
- Do they subscribe to magazines?
- Where do they live and how do they travel (which outdoor signs will they pass?).
- Do they use the internet or cable TV?
- Will you be 'pushing' products to distributors or creating 'pull' from customers?

Refer to your SWOT and PEST analysis.

Your plan

- How do you intend to make customers aware of your offer, remind them and make them buy?
- Remember your brand. Be consistent in how you apply it.
- Clearly define your budget. Be clear about how much you are willing to invest and what return you expect.
- Where you intend to advertise. Shop around. Check the audience they can deliver (target market reach).

Tread carefully!

The frequency of the message (how often do you need to run the advert) is the next thorny issue! Too few messages may result in low levels of awareness and understanding; too many exposures are wasteful and may turn-off your target audience.

You must also bear in mind seasonal patterns in consumer purchasing.

Use professional help if you need to – it's always better to have copy that works and delivers results than to waste money 'giving it a go'. Your campaign deserves to be professionally presented, supported by extra resources and expertise in order to ensure its success.

Working with agencies and suppliers

So much of marketing is collaborative. You will inevitably find yourself needing the help of all or any of the following – advertising, marketing communications, public relations, photographers, designers, marketing or business consultants to name but a few.

Do remember that these suppliers are also managing their own cash flow – ensure you pay in a timely fashion.

Treat your suppliers as partners – after all, you have chosen to work with them, now show them some respect!

Everyone can produce work in a hurry but you'll have a better time if you manage projects efficiently. Suppliers will charge you extra for rush jobs, so it really makes good sense to be prepared before you brief them.

Look for suppliers that you can work with for some time – each project they complete with you will make the next easier as they learn about your priorities, style of working, company culture, product range, etc.

Make time for suppliers. Introduce them to your team and provide them with a thorough brief at your first meeting.

Writing a brief

Providing a good brief will save you time and money, focus your mind and make you look good too!

The following generic list will help you cover all the salient points you should address.

1. Company profile.
2. Market overview.
3. Your objectives and description of task.
4. Audience/target market definition.
5. Budget.
6. Timescale.
7. Reporting requirements.
8. Existing information or examples of other work that is relevant.

Get buy-in for your brief from any interested parties before presenting it to your agency or supplier. You might have missed something and it will save red faces later!

Hot tip

Use the worksheet provided at the end of this book.

The A.I.D.A. principles

When either designing your own campaign or evaluating another, remember these four main factors of any successful advertisement:

Attention – you've got to grab the customer's attention! Make your headline compelling, tell your prospect what's in it for them. About 90% of the effectiveness of the advert is a result of the headline, so make it good!

Interest – now you've got them reading, make sure they stay for more! Follow your headline with more detail, keep the prospect hooked.

Desire – this is now the place for the list of benefits of your product or service. You're giving the prospect reasons for wanting what you have to offer…

Action – not only do you provide contact details but you need to tell the prospect to ring/write/fax NOW! Encourage immediate response before the advert just joins the 'to-do' pile.

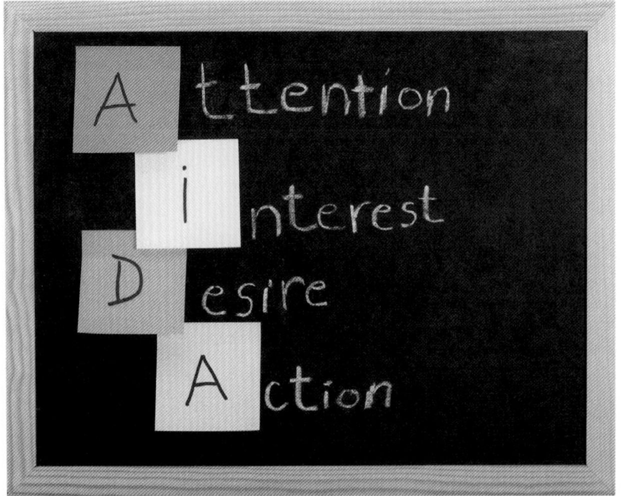

Dipping your toe in the water!

For a place to start when designing your campaign, why not try to sell more to your existing customers? After all, you should be able to take a lot of the guesswork out of who they are. Mine your data to see who bought what, when, and how often. Build a campaign around them.

Give me a sign, any sign!

Be bold and open your mind to both traditional and unusual places to advertise:

- Telephone directories
- Posters.
- Signs.
- Trains, buses, taxis, airports, company vehicles.
- Petrol pump nozzles, bumper stickers.
- Shopping bags, shopping trolleys.
- Leaflet drops.
- Inserts (loose and bound).

Hot tip

Also, see e-marketing on page 86 and Chapter 11.

Direct marketing

The production of direct mail tends to fall into four steps:

1. A mailing list of names and addresses.
2. The items to be mailed.
3. The resources to put your package together (stuffing).
4. Postal charges (size and weight).

Remember: 40% of all direct mail is discarded and 20% is never read! The average response rates are 7% for a consumer mailing and 6% for business to business.

Tips for success

1. Ensure you have a clear benefit in the headline.
2. Make a free offer.
3. Offer something extra if the customer acts immediately.
4. Include a free phone number.
5. Design a simple business reply card.
6. Plan which targets you will contact.
7. Tailor your message to each group.
8. Combine printed materials (postcards, letters, brochures, etc).

Hot tip

Most people do not appreciate telemarketing calls.

Ring, ring, won't you give me a call?

When telemarketing, beware the inappropriate phone call! Wrong time, wrong sort of customer, wrong offer, terrible script, incorrect customer information (contact has retired, left, vowed never to do business with you again), unintelligible telesales operator. Any of these are the kiss of death for your campaign.

However, good telemarketing can be extremely cost effective for generating inquiries and setting up sales calls. Be clear about your objectives and make sure your telemarketers are well trained and knowledgeable about your company and products.

Other areas that will negatively affect your campaigns are the length of time you take to respond to queries or follow up; the accuracy and user friendliness of your IT systems, and not having the necessary amount of time and people you need to keep the campaign moving.

Rubbish in, rubbish out

You do need to invest in an accurate database! Nowadays, customers expect you to contact them only when you have something relevant to tell them. None of us likes receiving mail or calls when our names are incorrectly spelt, job titles wrong, or the offer irrelevant – we can't help but think badly of the company that is wasting their money in this way.

Keep good campaign lists

- Check that bought-in lists are up to date.
- Keep your own in house lists clean.
- Ensure that any changes to the database are made regularly.
- If you are sent back undeliverable mail, take those details off the database immediately.
- Make someone responsible for the database – don't assume everyone cares about it as much as you do!
- Keep your lists relevant and your offers pertinent to the list.

e-marketing

E-marketing is the fastest growing form of marketing.

This is sometimes known as internet marketing and basically uses web and e-mail. It is a form of direct response marketing.

E-marketing includes search engine marketing (increases the visibility of websites in the search engine results page), e-mail marketing, interactive marketing (remembering what customers said last time and building on it), and viral marketing (providing incentives to consumers for passing on messages to friends and family).

E-marketing has 3 costs associated with it:

1. Development of a site.
2. Ongoing maintenance and hosting.
3. Marketing costs for the website.

You are likely to be measuring cost per response and cost per conversion.

Benefits to the customer include 24/7 access to websites, a significantly greater choice of suppliers and electronic catalogues (no paper), and comfortable shopping experience – all of which appeal to many consumers.

Benefits to you are that e-marketing may reduce the need for a sales force, thereby taking cost out of your organization, and it will definitely give you accurate user data with easy to measure response rates.

A recipe for success

1. Be aware of security concerns.
2. Pay attention to ways you can make the shopping experience feel less remote. Keep your site user-friendly and quick.
3. Remember that pricing needs to be well managed – information and comparison is available within seconds.
4. Provide money back, service, and quality guarantees.
5. Make sure you have an opt-in strategy for customers. Do not send unsolicited e-mails.
6. Let customers decide the format they prefer (HTML or plain text).
7. Be clear about your privacy policy. Promise not to sell or distribute customer information.
8. Include contact information and links. You may even want to provide links to other relevant sites.
9. Keep your content up to date.
10. Provide a rapid response (email or phone) to queries or complaints.
11. Send automated copies of orders to customers email address.
12. **PROOFREAD!**

Permission based e-mail marketing

Hot tip

See **Web Design In easy steps** for more on creating successful websites.

This is exactly what it says it is! It allows you to build a list of potential customers who want to hear from you. You will need a domain name, a capture page and an auto-responder.

A domain name is where your business can be found on the internet.

A capture page is the place on your website where your customers leave their details and sign up with you.

An auto responder allows you to store your pre-prepared e-mails and programme when they should be sent.

Public relations

PR is all about managing your company's reputation. Tools commonly used include press releases, press kits, product placement, webcasts, product launches, press conferences, establishing partnerships, and arranging events.

Hot tip

Keep tabs on all your marketing initiatives to ascertain what works for your company.

Good PR = sales growth!

If you have done something newsworthy and good with your product or service, you want to tell people so that they might be encouraged to buy from you.

If you have had a problem with your service or product, you'll want to demonstrate how you are working hard to make the situation better for existing customers. Hopefully this will encourage people to trust you and therefore continue to buy your product.

The most used form of PR is the press release.

Bear this in mind before you submit yours – everyone is having a bash so it had better be good! If you don't have the skills in-house, use an agency... a well written press release is more likely to catch the eye of the journalist you have targeted.

A poorly constructed press release will end up in the bin.

Was it worth it?

It is perfectly normal to use focus groups, surveys or interviews after a PR campaign to assess how effective it has been.

Don't forget your numbers – how much money is being spent in your budget and what are you getting for it? At the end of the year, you should be able to measure your results against the plan.

How your press release should look

Hot tip

Use the worksheet on page 177.

Your press release should be laid out simply and contain the following information:

- Name of contact.
- Company name.
- Telephone number.
- Fax number.
- E-mail address.
- Website address.

Ensure it is clearly marked PRESS RELEASE at the top, centre page in bold capitals.

- Headline.
- Opening paragraph (who, what, where, why).
- Then relevant product/service information and why your offering is unique.
- Quotes from relevant people (staff/industry experts/customers).
- Summary of story.
- Short company history.
- Clearly mark THE END.
- Press releases should be typed, double spaced in a basic format.
- Make sure each page is numbered.
- Check spelling and grammar.

What your press release should say

- First of all, be sure this story is actually worthy of a release!
- Your first ten words must grab attention.
- Make the story relevant to the paper or magazine you are sending the press release to. (Don't send product launch information unless it is genuinely part of a news story).
- Keep the press release factual, short and simple.
- Beware of jargon.
- Make sure you're contactable should the journalist want to discuss the story further.
- National coverage is hard to come by so it's a good idea to get to know the editors of all your local papers and magazines.
- Don't forget to put a copy of your press release on your own website – you may well create interest from unexpected quarters.
- Have photographs and sample products that support your press release ready for interested journalists.
- Don't hassle the journalists. Take it as read that if they haven't responded to your press release, they're not interested. They're busy and working to tight deadlines – your story just wasn't good enough this time!

Setting out your stall!

Exhibitions and trade shows are great for generating leads, meeting new customers, introducing new products and flag waving (to scare the competition!). Almost 50% of senior decision makers make purchase decisions at a show. Almost 80% of senior decision makers find at least one new supplier at the shows they attend. So it's worth fighting for their attention.

Exhibitions are also a great source of competitive information, so make time to get round all the stands. Watch their product demonstrations, collect literature, and make a note of the number of people manning the stand.

Should we, shouldn't we?

Before committing to stand space, check with the organizers who attended last year's show. You're looking for a high number of target customers in order to be sure that the investment is worthwhile.

When choosing where you want to have your stand, be prepared to pay for size (square footage) and location. If you have the choice, aim to be near the catering facilities – it will make it easier to cope with an overflow of customers on your stand and useful for staff who need to take a quick break without going too far!

Don't forget to organize pre-paid tickets for key customers and prospects.

Keeping up enthusiasm

Have a clear goal for your stand (number of visitors, value of orders taken, conversion rates) and ensure all your stand staff know! Set up some daily incentives – manning a stand can be very tiring and dull on quiet days, so try to spice things up with some targets and incentives.

The design of your stand

Try to make your stand eye-catching and worthy of spending time on. Demonstrate products and make sure there are things going on. You want people to stop and look and then be drawn onto the stand.

Sometimes stands are so intimidating that customers look and walk by which rather defeats the reason for being there. Keep the stand uncluttered and easy to walk about on. Avoid any barriers that prevent customers getting on or off.

Consider including a little cubby hole in your stand design. Make it large enough for bags and laptops to be kept securely, and ideally somewhere where someone can disappear to when they need to make or receive calls, complete any admin or have a drink of water.

Make their visit memorable

Offer literature and samples in a folder or bag so that the customer doesn't mislay it. Even better, take details and aim to have literature and samples shipped to their address before the exhibition is over.

Offer a prize draw of business cards and perhaps free novelty gifts for completing a registration form – then ensure the information is loaded onto your database!

Have premium gifts for your best customers or prospects. Make sure the gift is in keeping with your brand and theme. Keep them physically small, so that they aren't a pain to cart about.

How to survive an exhibition

1. Dress for a hard day on your feet.
2. Drink lots of water.
3. Carry some headache pills. Take regular short breaks to re-energize!
4. Make sure you have plenty of business cards.
5. Keep notes of interesting conversations and observations.

8 Princess Pee (Place)

Every morning in Africa a gazelle wakes up. It knows it must run faster than the fastest lion or it will be killed. Every morning a lion wakes up. It knows it must outrun the slowest gazelle or it will starve to death. It doesn't matter whether you are a lion or a gazelle – when the sun comes up, you'd better be running.

Anon

Princess Pee (Place)

Good working relationships with your distributors are also important.

Obviously, one of your main aims as a marketer is to make it easy for as many people as possible to buy your product. Unless you are a national retailer, it is extremely unlikely that you can do this on your own. At some point, you may have to look at using distributors or retailers to help you.

How to choose distributors

Your distribution channels should be defined by you once you know how your customers prefer to buy and if they already buy from preferred distributors.

You also know you to need to make your products or services easy to find in order to maximize sales, so you want good market coverage.

No doubt you also want to build good working relationships with your distributors, so it's worth checking out what their company culture and service levels are like. Life will be much more pleasant if you can work closely with your distributors, sharing responsibility for customer satisfaction without acrimony or blame.

It's worth considering which new distributors can offer you access to large target customers you haven't been able to reach.

What distributors want

Your channels want products that are easy to sell. They therefore want YOU to have created market demand which THEY can supply.

Distributors also want to make money. Your trading terms will have to reflect this (consider functional rebates and volume discounts). They will want a healthy return on their investment in your product.

Of course, distributors also want to be treated fairly. They will want support from you in terms of product training, marketing communications (many have their own catalogues and websites), and access to your entire product range.

They do not want to feel that one of their competitors (another distributor) is getting a better deal from you.

The first steps

Before you offer product to any channel, be sure that:

- It is ready to sell (no issues with quality, availability, demand, or pricing).
- You know what you want a distributor to do in terms of your working relationship.
- There is enough margin available to you and the distributor.

How many distributors do I need?

Much like a piece of string, the choice is yours!

Designing your distribution network is a balancing act. Among other things, you need to consider where your customers would like to buy your product; how much resource you have to work with distributors; where your competitors are selling product; whether you have margin available for both you and the distributor.

Of course, if you had only one product, you could match your distribution to the product life cycle, increasing the number of outlets as you move from introduction to decline. This can only work once for a start-up business – once you have an established distribution network, new products will be eagerly awaited by them all!

√

Direct v Distributors

In a business-to-business environment, a manufacturer may well prefer a direct relationship with the end user, for instance particularly when the account may be particularly demanding or when prices are so low that there isn't any margin left for a third party.

Some large accounts may also feel that it is more prestigious to be talking directly to the manufacturer.

(The downside of course, is that the manufacturer will be limited as to how far he can stretch his resources to support the end users.)

On the other hand...

This has to be set against the advantages distribution may offer to the customer, including –

- local sales/customer service/logistics support.
- an opportunity to bundle many products from one distributor thereby increasing discounts across the range.
- the ability to offer national support to multi-site accounts.

An expanded distribution network will also give you potential sales growth for minimal investment. Remember, it's your job to create the demand and it's the distributor's role to supply it.

Make sure you have the capacity to meet the increased demand though or you risk losing customers and distributors to a competitor's solution!

Network coverage

Your distribution network will give you the chance to get lots of your products as close to the customer as possible. It is worthwhile regularly reviewing your network to ensure you are getting the best coverage you can – make sure you're working with distributors who are well thought of and have a good reputation with customers.

Supporting your distributors

If resources allow it, allocate sales and customer service personnel to supporting your largest distributors. The closer you can work together, the better the level of customer service.

Bear in mind, channel support skills vary from those to support customers – for instance, inventory management, price management and sales promotion activity tend to be of key importance to distributors, whereas quality, problem resolution and training may well be more important to the end user.

Your sales reps should offer product training to distributors (and large end users). The distributor sales force has such a large number of products to offer and you must fight to get his attention. He is more likely to recommend products he knows and can present well.

Own label

Increasingly, national/large distributors are exploring dual-branding or own label possibilities. Be ready to deal with enquiries by addressing this in your strategic planning. Although the potential volumes may look inviting, be sure that by providing an own label you don't encourage end users to switch away from your branded product.

It may however offer you a great opportunity to extend the life cycle of a mature product while being able to move your sales and marketing people onto new product introductions!

Be prepared!

Never underestimate the negotiating power of a large, successful distributor!

Be prepared for your business reviews, have accurate information and treat them with respect.

Partnerships

A good relationship with a successful distributor is worth its weight in gold!

Make sure you recognize the value of what they do with you in your terms and conditions. The following suggestions are worthy of financial recognition –

- For instance, are they willing to share end user data with you, giving you another view of the customer?
- Are they also prepared to hold local inventory for your large key accounts?
- Will they commit to significant sales growth?
- Would they like a functional rebate scheme which rewards performance in areas you value?

However, I can't stress enough that there must be transparency in your terms and conditions. It's the only way to ensure a healthy relationship with individual distributors and the whole network.

Ensure they have a working relationship with their opposite numbers in your company – the better you all get along, the less confrontational any negotiations will be!

Be careful not to box yourself in a corner with a small number of large distributors who can then threaten to move business to your competitors.

Regularly review your channels to ensure you have product where the customer wants to buy it. This includes websites, catalogs and direct supply.

Also review the sales figures of your small distributors. Ensure it is not actually costing you your profit to get product to them. Consider asking large distributors to take them on as sub-distributors.

The e-auction – how it works

You might be tempted to put out or respond to a tender for business using an e-auction.

Once you have accepted, you'll be given a password and told when the auction is taking place. Usually you can see how many other companies are bidding and the price they're offering. The auction runs for a set amount of time, usually only hours. The best bid will win the business for an agreed period.

E-auctions are great if you're the buyer

You must be very specific about what you are wanting and for how long, but other than that, you can sit back and watch the suppliers you have chosen fight it out! You will also be able to specify whether you want branded or own label product.

Be a little cautious if you are the seller (or bidder)

Firstly, ensure you have done all your homework before the auction starts. Be clear about why you want this particular piece of business – do you want top line (sales) growth or bottom line (profit) contribution?

Be sure about the product specification and quantities. Check with manufacturing that the order won't cause any problems with stock levels or lead times.

Pay attention to packaging and delivery requirements. Again, it's easy to get caught out on the detail. Work out any costs associated with meeting the specification.

Most importantly, know what your lowest price can be and stick to it! I suggest you make sure there is someone at the computer with you during the auction – it can get very exciting and it's oh so tempting to just trim the price again (and again)... your colleague might just be able to prevent you giving away all your margin!

Summary

- Review and select the best routes to market for your product – for instance, direct or indirect, online or wholesale, a combination of a few
- Remember, different market segments might require different routes!
- Don't assume your competitors have got it right!
- Focus on routes to market that make you money! Your business has to be able to afford whichever route you select
- Use your market research to inform your decision
- Confirm trading terms whichever route(s) you select
- Support your distribution network or alternative route with product training, joint calls to end users (where appropriate), competitive pricing, samples, customer service

All the little Pees (Process, People)

Make it simple. Make it memorable.

Make it inviting to look at.

Make it fun to read.

Leo Burnett

All the little Pees

Supply chain management refers to managing the flow of goods initiated by a customer order, from raw materials to suppliers through to the manufacturer who then passes finished goods out to a distributor/wholesaler and to the retailer and customer.

Increasingly, marketers will take a very active role in this whole process. All organizations, irrespective of size, will have some kind of supply chain.

The overall objective is to reduce the amount of inventory in the pipeline between suppliers, manufacturers, wholesalers, distributors, retailers and customers, without adversely affecting customer satisfaction or profitability.

There are 6 key elements of a supply chain:

1. Production – making the product.
2. Supply – knowing what product to make.
3. Inventory – having enough product.
4. Location – product in the best place.
5. Transportation – moving the product around.
6. Information – knowing what's happening.

There are 3 main areas of focus:

1. The product flow involves the movement of goods along the supply chain between suppliers, manufacturers and customers. It includes inventory, scheduling, transportation, and any returns from the customer.
2. The information flow focuses on the orders and delivery notification.
3. The finance flow is made up of credit terms, payment, and consignment details.

Get out your crystal ball!

As a marketer, you will be expected to make a significant contribution in the area of product flow, particularly demand forecasting (new products, promoted products, quality issues affecting sales and product switching, competitive activity, sales incentives, distributor marketing activity, changes to the distribution network, and significant customer or market events).

You need to give some thought as to how you can regularly gather realistic forecast data that can be fed back into manufacturing to ensure appropriate inventory levels!

One answer can be to gather together a cross functional team on a monthly basis to share information and review results. The team should include senior representatives from manufacturing, customer services, accounting, marketing, sales and logistics.

Each member of the team should bring information to the table which can help to explain the reasons behind problems already experienced and also give input for forecasts based on market knowledge.

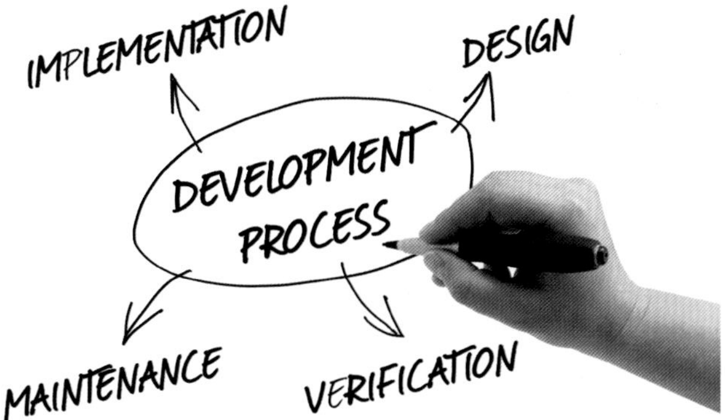

Process, process, process

Supply chain management (SCM) will inevitably drive the introduction and management of processes. Getting the best from your supply chain relies on collaborative work between functions, suppliers, distributors and customers, so processes have to be developed to ensure accurate and timely shared information is available.

You'll find yourself using words like workflow, optimization and process mapping on a horribly regular basis!

Improving existing processes

Beware

Not everyone can adopt to changes easily – so be prepared for some resistance.

1. Review existing processes on flow charts.
2. Keep asking why things are done the way they are.
3. Identify and discard the steps which don't add value.
4. Manage any changes you make.
5. Get feedback after changes have been made.
6. Celebrate successful changes.
7. Record and learn from changes that have been made or try again if the environment has changed.

Change management

It is quite probable that your company will face major change at least once in every three years. It is extremely likely that marketing will be heavily involved. Causes of change include the need for growth, competitor or customer pressure, and a new business strategy.

Do not embark on any change program lightly! Try not to underestimate the effect of insufficient training, poor communications, ineffective leadership and poor project management skills.

More than half of all change programs fail so make sure that the right systems are in place to support new work practices. There is a wealth of experience about change, so using some tried and tested wisdom is a good place to start.

...cont'd

The Chartered Institute of Personnel and Development have also produced a robust model based on their research –

1. Choose a team.
2. Craft the vision and the path.
3. Connect organization wide change.
4. Consult stakeholders.
5. Communicate.
6. Cope with change.
7. Capture learning.

John P. Kotter's model for successful change provides a tremendous checklist:

1. Increase urgency (inspire people to move).
2. Build the guiding team (bring together the right mix of skills).
3. Get the vision right (articulate a simple vision and strategy).
5. Communicate for buy-in (involve everyone).
6. Empower action (remove obstacles, collect feedback).
7. Create short term wins (keep tasks in bite size chunks).
8. Don't let up (keep on track).
9. Make change stick (weave change into the culture).

Initiative or improvement?

Think carefully about whether you're really managing a change initiative or a process improvement – people get weary of continual change programs and will stop listening.

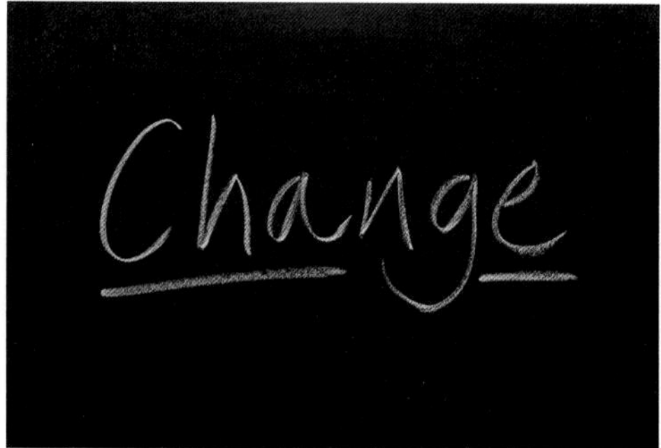

Caution – change occurring!

Watch out for resistance to change from either individuals or groups. This can be caused by a variety of emotions including a loss of control, shock of the new, uncertainty, inconvenience, a threat to status, and fear of inability to do the new job.

You can avoid having your project derailed by paying attention to what is going on around you and ensuring the right amounts of time and support are in place.

Leading change, or taking responsibility for making change happen, can be exhausting. Ensure you have great support in the office (mentor, coach, trusted colleague) and at home (without laboring the point, make sure family members understand what you're working to achieve and by when). Get away from the project at regular intervals to allow your brain a breather.

Look for small wins on the way. Celebrate success. Give credit where credit is due and make people feel involved.

Don't forget to tell people what you are going to do, what you are doing, and what you have done!

Make sure you've got the involvement and support of senior managers and opinion leaders in the company. Their influence, demonstrated by what they say and do, will make many people more receptive to change. So invite your heavyweights to all your big presentations and ask them to make the opening speeches.

10 Come closer, come closer

Trends, like horses, are easier to ride in the direction they are going.

John Naisbitt

Sales

Sales and marketing are not the same thing. If marketing is an octopus, sales are one of the tentacles! Both are inextricably linked.

Effective marketing will make the sales function more efficient. It is a marketing responsibility to ensure that the sales function is fully supported and listened to but it is also OK to disagree with your reps providing you have the evidence to back up your point of view!

Customers want to see reps for many reasons – reassurance, training and problem solving among them – so you should ensure that the sales force have the information and confidence to be credible.

Get out of the office!

Write up a short report capturing your observations and customer or sales feedback. Highlight action points and dates by which you will have met any commitments you've agreed to. Circulate this to the sales rep, sales manager and marketing group.

The sales process

1. Know the product or service.
2. Find and qualify sales leads.
3. Initial contact.
4. Sales presentation.
5. Propose solutions/handle objections.
6. Close the sale.
7. Service and follow-up.

Beware 

After-sales service is just as important as Step 2. Often, Step 7 is neglected by organizations, leading to loss of customer loyalty.

Keep them coming back

The sales process, as defined in the seven steps above, is actually circular rather than a list. After all, we all want our customers to come back for more of our product line or services!

Each company's sales process will take a different amount of time to complete. A general rule of thumb is that the higher the value of the goods and services, the greater the time taken from qualification to closing the sale.

Your challenge is to imagine what tools or new approaches might speed up the sales process – after all, it is in everyone's best interest to identify, win and keep happy customers as quickly as possible!

Good housekeeping

Think about the costs associated with each of the steps in the process. See where you can add value either by speeding up the time it takes to complete the process (for instance, by generating quality leads that are well qualified before being handed over to the rep) or by ensuring another part of the organization can take responsibility for managing parts of the process in a more cost effective manner (for example, making regular customer service telephone calls to key customers rather than sales visits).

Get creative!

Matching skills to jobs.

Step 2 of the sales process may be more efficiently addressed with sales support activity – after all, finding and qualifying sales leads can be done using good lists and a telephone.

Your reps are an expensive resource and not necessarily best equipped to create and trawl through lists of prospects. Consider using someone with a good telephone manner to qualify leads before handing them over to the rep.

Arguably, the sales rep is best used for steps 3-6 of the sales process – he/she is generally the most effective method of acquiring new customers. Once the relationship is established, you may well be able to hand the day to day management (or retention) of the account to customer services or sales support.

Try setting up a small team to work with the process before rolling it out across the whole sales and customer service group. Learn from their experience and customer feedback.

We all have a part to play

Marketing should make a significant contribution towards speeding up the sales process, particularly by getting the sales rep in front of the customer.

Ask yourself whether you are providing the sales arm of your company with the best training, product information, hot (qualified) leads, and presentation aids.

- Are you monitoring delivery and customer service issues?
- Do you have contact with your biggest and best customers?

Sales force automation

Guaranteed to send a shiver down the backs of many sales reps, this term refers to using websites and technology to improve the capability and effectiveness of your sales force.

Automation will offer you the chance to bring customer history into one place and provide a common view across the company. It should also speed up customer response times and reduce the cycle time of placing orders.

Start small

Beware complex software and a feeling of Big Brother management practices! Keep implementation simple by building contact information over time. Invest in training so that sales people feel they can add value.

Customer services

Anyone responsible for customer services needs a good telephone manner, active listening skills, the ability to create trust and rapport, good problem solving skills, and the ability to defuse anger.

Working hand-in-hand with sales, your customer services team are responsible for keeping existing customers. They need visibility of your customers and the authority to take action if there's a problem brewing. Close contact with the sales function will ensure that together they can take responsibility for managing customer satisfaction.

It's definitely worth exploring incentives and rewards that recognize the vital contribution this function makes to the ongoing health of the business. Sometimes it's possible to hand over the day to day management of existing customers to customer services, thereby freeing up sales time to focus on getting new business.

Get customer service people out to key accounts. Encourage relationship building at several key points in the customer organization. These working relationships might just save the day in times of crisis.

Back to basics

Check that anyone responsible for your customer services is consistently working to a high standard. Make sure you're familiar with their measurements of success. After all, good customer service can give you a competitive advantage. Bad customer service is a gift to your competitors.

Hot tip

Use the worksheet on page 179 to determine the appropriate level of support for each customer group.

Signs of excellent customer service

Beware

Dissatisfied customers will almost definitely be lost forever, but, the bad experience will also be talked about in coffee breaks and dinner parties!

1. The phone is answered within three rings.
2. Promises made to customers are kept.
3. Customers are listened to carefully.
4. Your customer services team can identify existing customers with access to sales history data.
5. Complaints are dealt with promptly using the company complaints procedure.
6. Customer services personnel are helpful and prepared (and empowered) to use their own initiative in order to delight your customers.

Customer feedback

Beware

Don't ask for their feedback during each call. Keep a log of each time the customer is asked and whether they obliged or declined.

1. Ask your customers on a regular basis how they rate your customer service.
2. Find out what their expectations are and be clear about who your benchmark competitor is.
3. Measure the number of complaints you receive and the time it takes to resolve them.
4. Work really hard to turn disgruntled customers into loyal customers.
5. Make it easy for customers to give feedback and use a standard feedback form.

CRM (Customer Relationship Management)

Used particularly by direct marketers and to support the sales process, CRM refers to the use of computerized databases for:

1. The collection and organization of data (prospects, customers, product, sales, competitors).
2. Planning, scheduling and integrating customer development activities and communications.
3. The analysis and reporting of all sales related activities and data.

It is well accepted that it costs a business more to find new customers (acquire) rather than keep (retain) existing customers. So it is very important to develop processes which are about maximizing retention (based on customer services) and another set of processes for acquiring new customers (based on sales and marketing services).

One of the huge advantages of a computerized database is the customer visibility given to all functions across an organization. For instance, if your customer services group can see when the customer was last visited, what they bought and so on, they are more likely to be able to provide good support. They might resolve the problem, delight the customer, take an order, and save a sales call!

The emperor's new clothes

Beware spending too much on a computerized system that is far too sophisticated for your needs. It will also tie up your staff in training, data collection and management time. It's tempting to design a bespoke (made to measure) system but it's very likely that an off the shelf package will do everything you want, particularly in the early days…

So before you buy anything, think carefully about what information you want out of the system and what you will do with it. Plot your workflows. This will save you money, energy and embarrassment! Start small and get your data collection processes right first. See what marketing you can do with this database. With the hard work done, it will be easier to transition to a more powerful solution at the right time.

Return on investment (ROI)

Increasingly, marketers are asked to justify their activities in terms of ROI. This becomes more important the more you spend! Basically, ROI measures how effectively the firm uses its capital to generate profit; the higher the ROI, the better.

You may well find that you will be expected to provide an ROI calculation to develop a business case for a given proposal. ROI is usually stated as a % over a specific time (often 3 years for IT projects). It involves knowing what to measure and understanding how to quantify the value of those measurements into actual pounds.

This is the perfect time to find your accountant!

Lay good foundations

In order to make life easier, start each project that involves investment (money, time, resources) with good baseline data.

Be sure you're collecting the right data – once these points are firmly fixed in the measurement process, you can't go back in a year or two's time and wish you'd measured something else!

Be clear about your definition of success and get agreement to those numbers before you start! Otherwise you run the risk of spending far too much time searching for a measure that makes everyone happy once the project is underway.

It is good marketing practice to understand what difference your activities are making to the profit and loss sheet.

Stating the obvious

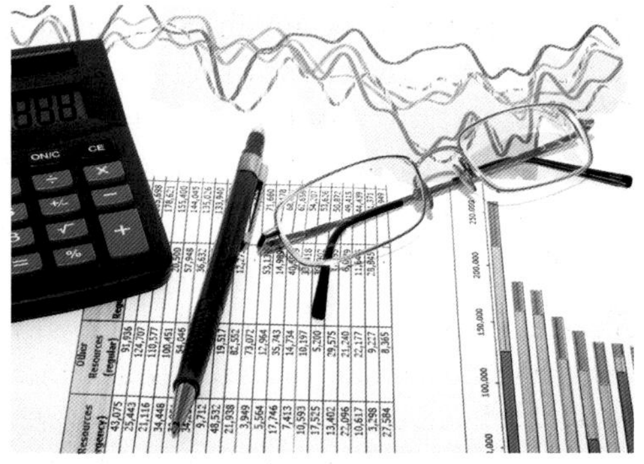

You will inevitably be asked to cut back on marketing spend at some time, usually when sales take a dip, and you'll be able to be much more responsive if you are already measuring the success of your activities. By being able to identify which marketing activity delivers the greatest return, you'll also be able to see where less profitable activity can be cut.

Measurement

As a marketer, it is important to be able to evaluate success, monitor progress, compare performance, and drive good behavior. Whatever you feel is appropriate to measure given your business, be systematic and consistent in your approach.

As your business changes, review what you're measuring. Make sure it's still appropriate.

What tends to be measured in businesses today:

1. Customer satisfaction.
2. Customer retention.
3. Customer loyalty.
4. Customer profitability.
5. Customer acquisition and conversion.
6. Length of customer relationships.
7. Customer lifetime value.

Focusing

"Not everything that counts can be measured, and not everything that can be measured counts."

Albert Einstein

Make sure your measurements are focused around your business objectives. It's easy to get carried away and start measuring new things every month, but you'll drown in data and not have an established baseline to work against!

Use your measures for positive outcomes wherever possible. After all, you want everyone to succeed. People will be supportive of metrics if they are cause for some celebration or recognition of a job well done but are likely to start fudging data if it makes life easier.

Hot tip 

KISS – time consuming and over-the-top systems will waste time as well as resulting in your staff losing interest in the data.

A simple system

Try not to be too ambitious with the variety of things you want from your CRM system. You'll just be adding expense to the design and making it more complicated for the users.

You should aim to produce data that tells you…

- Who bought what, when, and how much they spent.
- How often they buy from you.
- Who has responded to your marketing communications.
- What customers are using, if it's not your product or service.
- Which customers are most profitable.

Opportunity Analysis in 10 minutes

1. Rank your customers 3 ways – who has bought most recently, who has bought most often, and who has spent the most with you.

2. For each group, give the company/name at the top a score of 1, the second, a 2, and so on.

3. Now add the scores by customer across the three groups. Those with the total lowest scores (i.e. most often at the top of each group) are your key customers.

4. Ideally, you should now focus your marketing efforts behind the companies at the top of your list. Don't ignore the others, just understand that your greatest opportunity is likely to be with the companies at the top.

RFM

Recency, Frequency, Monetary Value is a profiling tool.

Recency is the number of months since the last purchase and is used to predict response to any subsequent offer. Basically, the longer ago your customer bought something from you, the harder it will be to get them to purchase again.

Frequency is the number of purchases made either in a specific time frame or total value. Again, customers who buy from you often are more likely to continue.

Monetary value is the total amount spent with you. It can relate to a specific time frame or total spend. It is the least useful in predictive modeling.

Customer satisfaction

Apparently, unhappy customers each tell up to 10 people about their dissatisfaction. They are extremely unlikely to complain to their supplier or manufacturer (about 90% of customers say nothing), which makes it very difficult to put things right before the customer has walked away and also disenchanted several potential customers. You must make sure that –

1. Customers are encouraged to complain.
2. You can resolve these complaints very quickly.
3. You regularly review complaints to make changes and reduce the causes of dissatisfaction.

Customer satisfaction and retention walk hand-in-hand

High levels of complaints are an indicator that you are losing customers. Remember, it's more expensive to find customers than to keep them – in the interests of growth and profit you should work hard to delight your existing customer base!

If you see the numbers of complaints rising dramatically, pay attention! Make time to review the causes of these complaints so that you can identify whether it is failing processes or personnel issues that are the problem.

Always ensure you're available to talk to some of the unhappy customers – take personal ownership for problem resolution and attempt to turn negative customer opinion to a positive one.

How to make an impact!

Rather than be overwhelmed by the scale of the task ahead of you, concentrate your efforts on the following –

1. Precision targeting – identify the most important customers.

2. Campaign excellence – optimize the marketing campaign process from targeting through to execution.

3. Loyalty management – develop specific experiences for each customer segment that are unique to customers and their specific needs.

Customer insight

The main objective of customer insight roles or departments is to build profitable long term relationships with your customers (and you can add suppliers and employees).

One aim is use any information you hold on databases to enable you to meet customer needs without wasting time and money repeatedly asking the same questions.

If you, or a colleague, are given the responsibility of customer insight you will be expected to –

1. Identify meaningful customer segments, customer needs and expectations.
2. Examine processes and functions to ensure they are customer-centric.
3. Encourage and enable your company to focus entirely on the customer.
4. Implement actions to improve the customer experience.
5. Measure internal performance, customer behavior and customer perception to determine what further action is required.

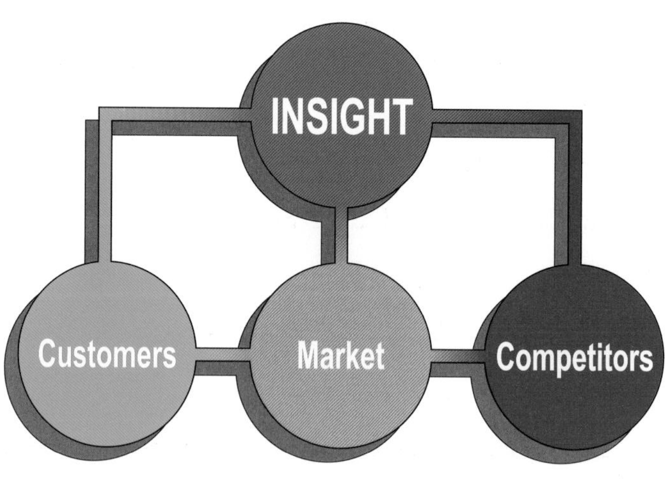

Call centres

Nowadays, call centres tend to be large relatively quiet areas (you'll rarely hear phones ringing) full of headset-wearing staff, working at terminals. There is often a large electronic display board on the wall showing the number of calls waiting to be answered (queuing) and how long the queue is in minutes.

Increasingly, the call centre will be equipped with automated attendant technology which directs customers to different areas ("press 1 for technical help, press 2 for customer services", etc). Sometimes this is managed with speech recognition software.

Call centres can be dealing with inbound calls (providing technical support, answering customer queries for example) and/or making outbound calls (sales or market research).

Well-run call centres provide their agents with...

- Training (usually for each call type).
- Guides (for each call type).
- Information (easy to find and clearly presented).
- Good working environment.

Spend a day in your call centre and have a look at their scripts/guides. Ask if there is anything you can add/provide to make the calls run more smoothly.

Hot tip

See the worksheet on page 180.

Time for a disguise!

Hot tip

Ring your call centre to test whether you enjoy the experience.

Do a little mystery shopping of your own and ring your call centre (or one that you intend to use to represent your business) to get a slice of customer experience.

When you do so, make notes and answer the following –

1. Who answers the phone?
2. Do they do so happily?
3. Do they clearly identify the company and give their name?
4. Are they knowledgeable?
5. Do they speak clearly and avoid slang or jargon?
6. Do they deal with the customer efficiently?
7. Do they phone back if they promise to?
8. Do they know who rang and collect contact details?
9. What happens if the line is busy? Does the call bounce to someone else or is the customer potentially lost?
10. Is there consistency in the way phone calls are dealt with?

Customers calling you want something. You need to take good care of these people! They are 'hot' prospects/leads. Now you have the opportunity to wow them…

11 Online, On time!

"You can't just ask customers what they want and then try to give that to them. By the time you get it built, they'll want something new."

Steve Jobs, CEO Apple

Online, on time!

In addition to the brief overview of e-marketing in Chapter 7, this guide would not be complete without exploring web based activity in more detail.

Having an online presence has become an essential part of marketing your business. Whether you are a sole trader or huge company, your customers will expect to find some evidence of your existence on the internet.

How do I do it?

First of all, decide what your site is for. Do you want to use it as a way of signposting your existence or drawing customers in to your online "shop"? Will you be limiting your presence to a certain geography or demographic? Will you be able to keep your website updated regularly and resourced adequately? Can you back up any promises you make in your online campaign?

Budget

Again, how much you invest can be as long as a piece of string – a rough guide is to allow up to 20% of your total marketing spend on your website.

Your website may well be your main presence in the market. It is critical that it represents your company well. Customers are increasingly sophisticated – a clunky site may send them running into the arms of your competitors. So seriously consider buying in the expertise of a design firm.

It's all in the name!

Ideally, your domain name or URL should be the same as your company or as close as possible. Keep it relevant to your product or services and check that it isn't too similar to someone else's.

The name isn't yours until it is registered, so once you've checked that it is not already being used (search via 'domain names'), you should select a provider and place your order! It isn't expensive so you should DEFINITELY invest in all the main extensions (.org; .com; .co.uk; .net for example) and alternative spellings of your address.

A Warm Welcome

Once your name is working, visitors will (hopefully) come flocking to your site! Be a good host – welcome your guests in and get their details in your visitor's book...or in other words, ensure that your web reports tell you what you want to know about the people who found your site. Where did they come from? Which search engines are working best for you? Where did they go and what did they look at? How long did they stay? How many completed a purchase and filled a basket but didn't buy? Which day or at what times is there most traffic on your website?

Do use e-mail creatively to support your website. It is a powerful one-to-one communication and keeps a dialogue open between you and your customer. Consider sending an e-mail after an order is placed, on its way or delivered to reassure the customer; a follow up e-mail to check if you can offer help with an unfinished order or provide any after sales service. Autoresponders (a scheduled e-mail) can be an effective way of keeping in touch with your customer base.

Do not send junk e-mails ("spam"). Never, ever. Only use lists of people who have already given their permission to be contacted. Adopt a double opt-in strategy (the customer enters his e-mail address in order to subscribe and you sent him a confirmation e-mail with a link back to your site) so that you can avoid any accusations of spamming.

Do remember to include contact details on all your communications. A postal address is essential in the US.

Don't use dodgy lists - be sure they are from reputable sources. Keep your lists up to date and remove addresses that are no longer live.

Do allow customers to opt out at any time – if they want to be taken off your lists, do so IMMEDIATELY and confirm by e-mail that you have done so. Not only is it good manners, it's also the law!

Beware

Beware falling foul of the law – be familiar with Email Marketing Law in your country or region (USA Can-Spam Act 2003 supersedes individual laws of the 36 states and takes an opt-out approach). UK/Europe law requires prior consent (opt-in) or an existing customer relationship, clear identification of the sender and an address in order to withdraw consent).

Hot tip

Research suggests that customers are most receptive to e-marketing activity on Tuesday and Wednesday....so test this out with yours! Also, avoid running campaigns during holidays – guess where your customers are?!

Walking the Talk

We've probably all been caught by websites that fail to deliver on their promises. Slow sites, misleading information, stock that is ordered back to back resulting in long lead times, shipping errors and damaged goods will ensure you get little repeat business.

DO be clear about who your customers are and what they want. Traditional marketing principles still apply to all your e-marketing activity.

DO brand and customise your site in line with the rest of your company communications. Be consistent.

DON'T leave your website unattended – however small your presence, regularly check that your "shop window" is still relevant, well maintained and attractive. Use good photographs, animation and videos to show product or simplify information.

DON'T forget to check out your competitor's websites too – your customers probably will be. Find out whether they have a presence on MySpace or YouTube. Read their testimonials. Pay attention to the details.

DO work to increase traffic to your site. Put the address on all your communication tools from letter headings to pencils and keyrings; create links between your website and other relevant sites; invest in a search engine submission service; ensure your site can deal with the vast majority of enquiries, like frequently asked questions.

Hot tip

TRACK what you do. MEASURE what you get. What is your bottom line? HOW can you improve your results next time?

Commonly used terms for metrics are –

E-mail Deliverability – how much of your opt-in e-mail is actually being delivered? Is it for instance, being caught in spam filters?

Open rates – how many of your opt-in e-mails are actually being opened? Almost half of all e-mails sent are not seen by the customer! Check the accuracy of your list, the attractiveness of your greeting, make sure your communication doesn't look like spam… these are just a few of the factors that could adversely affect your open rates.

Click-Through Rates – So your e-mail has arrived and been opened but will the customer chose to click through to your site? Is your offer attractive and have you targeted the right customer group?

Click-to-Conversion Rates – How many of your customers have responded in the way you hoped? This could be a sale, an enquiry form, a request for samples or product demonstration for example…

"Hey, have you heard...?"

Hot tip

Don't forget to ensure your campaign is resourced flexibly as it may start small but will potentially explode in terms of numbers. You MUST be in a position to respond.

Even in e-marketing, some old sayings still remain true. For instance, there is still nothing as powerful as personal recommendation and good news travels fast. Welcome to viral marketing!

Assume every adult has about a dozen friends and you can find something interesting to say to yours, who in turn pass it on to theirs, then you have started your very own viral marketing campaign. Even better if you can find a way of encouraging people or companies to use your material as part of their own communications strategy and then they are working on your behalf!

Sometimes referred to as "word-of-mouse"," buzz", "network" or "word-of-blog" marketing, viral marketing is here to stay. As marketing budgets get squeezed, this is one way of making less money go further.

Not all campaigns will work. Common sense suggests many won't. But just think of the impact of the viral campaign that flies – the ones we have had to see!

Aim to keep your message short and snappy, easily passed around and memorable. Entertain the viewer. Many of us still remember the dancing baby – he had to be seen to be believed! Invest in a YouTube account and experiment with short videos (ideally no longer than two minutes). Get creative and remember the best examples of viral marketing are not necessarily the most expensive. Have a story and tell it well.

This is a perfect illustration of a viral marketing campaign that takes on a life of its own. The following story was originally found in a regional paper, the Northern Echo. It was then picked up by a UK national paper, The Sunday Times. "A great-grandmother is an internet sensation after securing her first acting job at the age of 82. Jean Jones has been watched more than 500,000 times on YouTube after starring in an advert for Aldi. "I buy this tea for my husband," she tells viewers. "He likes tea. I don't like tea. I like gin." Mrs Jones said: "When I was in the post office the girl behind the counter asked for my autograph." No doubt, this advert will have been watched many more times by the end of its life.

Social Networks

Businesses of all sizes can find a fit with social networks like Facebook, Twitter, YouTube, MySpace, Hi5 and LinkedIn. It can be a great (and cost effective) way to increase awareness and grow sales.

Many of your customers are already users of these sites – it's a great way to get a dialogue going with your target audience! You can invite them to your pages, to comment on your products or service and to recommend you to their friends and family. You can build your brand, develop your own community and leverage the networks of key influencers. Always link your website to your social networks… in fact, link anything that you feel may be of interest to your fellow networkers!

Hot tip

Each social network has its own etiquette and language. If you aren't a regular user, take the time to become familiar with how the groups communicate and what is well received…

Some tasty stats!

Don't forget

Keeping your page or group fun and edgy can also be time consuming. If you encourage comment, someone has to respond in order to keep the conversation going. Your network needs something to talk about to keep you relevant...

The average (if there is such a thing) Facebook user has 130 friends and is connected to 60 pages, groups and events! More than half of Facebook users are over 25 years old and 55% are women. More than 100 million users access Facebook through a mobile device. 25 billion pieces of content are shared each month via Facebook – so there is both room and scope for you!

Twitter gets more than 300,000 new users every day and over 60% of use is outside the US. At the moment, 110 million people use Twitter and there are more than 600 million searches every day!

YouTube boasts 2 billion viewers per day, is available in 19 countries and 12 languages, and uploads 24 hours of video every minute! More than 50% of users are under 20 years old. YouTube also boasts the second largest search engine in the world.

So social networks can open up new markets and new customer groups to you...

Using the social networks own search engine can be a great way to find out what people are saying about your business. Interesting market research, current and low cost!

So what's the catch?

You will have to steer clear of corporate speak and suits! You will get the best results if you can show that your business is friendly and engaging. Your objective has to be to keep it fun and entertaining (after all, it is SOCIAL networking!) Post photos, stream video and start a debate. If you do it right, this can also be the perfect place to go viral...

Avoid advertising in the traditional way – this is a different beast! Listen and respond to your network, give them something to talk about.

"Call me...or better still, TEXT!"

Who doesn't have a cell phone? Chances are high that your customers all do and there's plenty of research that suggests the vast majority of us see SMS texting as the phone's most important feature. In Britain, the average user sends over 1200 texts a year!

BUT before you launch a cell phone marketing campaign do be sure that your customers really would appreciate hearing from you in this way! This sounds obvious but make sure it is an appropriate medium for your target groups.

DO integrate your cell phone marketing campaign with all your marketing activity.

DO consider enlisting the help of experts to source lists of numbers and send the messages. You will also be given campaign feedback which will help you improve the next one!

DO explore pull messages rather than push messages - encourage the customer to respond to your offer.

DO brace yourself for an immediate and high response – if your offer is good, customers will let you know very quickly. Seriously consider how you will manage customer response and resource appropriately.

DO NOT forget the principles of permission based marketing – your cell phone campaign has to meet the same legal requirements as your e-mail activity.

DO respect your customers' privacy and only contact them with something you believe is relevant. Ensure they can opt out, usually by texting back 'STOP' or similar.

DO make use of geographic targeting – GPS technology makes this easier than ever. It may also allow you to roll out a campaign and manage response rates effectively.

Summary

There are many advantages to investing in online marketing activity with the huge variety of online options available – flexibility, targeting your message to customer segments, tracking results in real time – but tailor your online activity to the resources you have available.

- Integrate not only your communication tools with your website but also all your online and off line marketing activity.
- Treasure your database- keep it clean and accurate.
- Apply traditional business principles to your e-marketing activity.
- Ban spam!
- Explore viral campaigns if they are pertinent to your customer base and within your capabilities...
- Check out the relevance of social network marketing and cell phone campaigns to your marketing activity....if you're not already trying it out, consider how many people you know that DON'T have a phone...not many are there?
- Finally, stay within the law!

"By creating conversation, we let our customers spread our message by word of mouth."

Anita Roddick

Simply the best!

Every word, sentence, and headline should have one specific purpose – to lead your potential customer to your order page.

Shelley Lowert

Communication

Hot tip 

You may want to use **Giving Great Presentations in easy steps.**

As a marketer, you will spend a huge amount of time communicating to (you hope!) interested parties. Work hard to match your message to your audience – remember that people generally have an extremely small attention span, so don't overwhelm them with information that isn't relevant.

Support any presentation with handouts so that your audience can concentrate on what you're saying rather than on taking notes. Condense visual information into bullet points – they're far easier to retain and will have more impact than huge chunks of text.

Pay attention to detail when you write. Edit and proofread everything! Check for spelling mistakes and repetition. Avoid using the same word over and over. Use grammar and spell checking software, even on e-mails.

Ask a colleague to look over what you've written to see if it makes sense or, even better, read your work out loud to a small group before going public. Invite feedback and make changes where necessary.

Project Management

If you don't plan to plan, plan to fail!

Make sure your plans support the business goals. It sounds obvious but it's not unheard of for marketers to ignore agreed business objectives in favor of following their own hunches or pet projects.

If your strategy is robust, the marketing planning cycle will get easier each year as you'll be on track and just fine tuning the detail.

What is the plan for?

The only reason any plan exists is to give clear direction to those who need it. It is basically your map, showing where you are, where you want to go and what the conditions are likely to be during your journey.

So keep your plan visible and refer to it often. Don't be afraid to make changes where necessary and draw everyone's attention to alterations. This way you keep your plan alive and relevant.

Using what you have

So much of your planning work is really about managing your resources. You only have a limited budget and number of people to allocate to projects in order to achieve your goals, so treat them as the precious resources they are!

Tick, tock

Ensure your timescales are realistic and don't make any promises you may not be able to keep! Save yourself the embarrassment of eating humble pie as yet another product launch misses its deadline, by building in sufficient time to complete tasks into your plans.

Hot tip

See **Project Management in easy steps.**

Plan B

Always have a contingency in place – developing scenarios of things that could go wrong and how you'll get projects back on track is time well spent.

Involve colleagues from as many functions as possible in this and don't forget to look at past plans. You and your team members may already have learned invaluable lessons and you'll come to projects wiser and more effective if you build on these.

A little bit at a time

Break large projects down into smaller chunks and put in place deadlines for each of these. This way, you should be able to keep the whole project on time even if various tasks go a little awry.

Attention, please!

When something changes that will affect your plan, let all those involved know. If you miss deadlines, find out why, communicate and use this when developing your next plan.

The A-team

Make sure you have the right team to deliver the plan. Be clear about the skills, knowledge and competencies needed. Then identify the individuals. Don't be tempted to select your favorites to work with – it might be more fun initially, but will put the plan at risk.

I see you

Think about what support they might need as they work on the project. Who can provide this?

Pay attention to whether certain individuals are more heavily loaded than others – it's too easy to select people for teams because they're great to work with and then see them becoming stressed and less effective through over work. Meanwhile, someone else has time on their hands to make their contribution look absolutely stunning!

Keep a handle on which plans are on the go. If you have the space, chart them on your wall with team member's names so that you can identify any timeline or resource issues.

Use SMART objectives

Specific – what do you actually want to achieve?

Measurable – how will you measure whether you are meeting the objectives or not?

Achievable – are the objectives actually possible?

Realistic – do you have the resources to achieve the objective?

Timeline – when are you going to do this by?

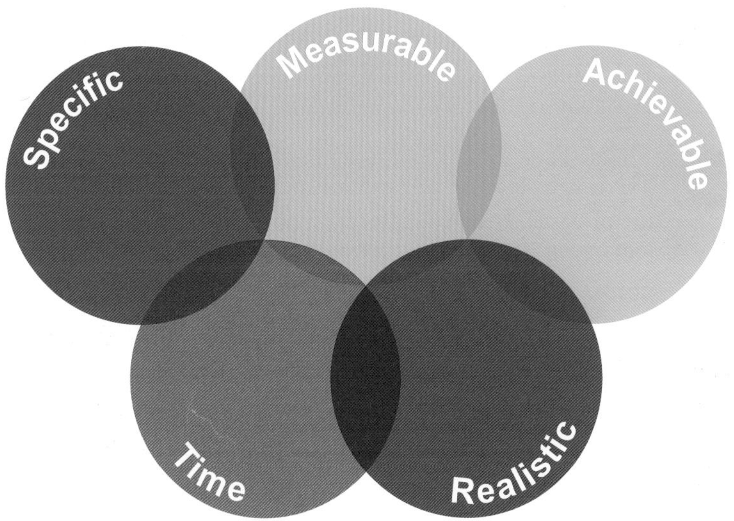

Use SMART Worksheet at the back of the book.

Team-working

It may seem easier to disappear into an office for a few days and then make an entrance clutching all the answers in your hand. Don't be tempted to do this. Use the resources around you to work on problems – it might seem to slow things down but actually the time spent at the beginning will save you time and energy defending your solutions.

1. At the beginning of the task, write a plan (sound familiar?).
2. Agree the aims of the group (this may take longer than you think – this is almost the hardest bit). Make sure everyone is clear about what you have agreed to do.
3. Try not to let any one person dominate (yes, that may mean you!). Involve different people in time keeping, collecting ideas on the white board, facilitating, taking notes.
4. Do your best to play to team members' strengths – let people use their skills.
5. Make sure you keep checking that all the team members are committed.
6. Don't be afraid to constructively challenge the team or individuals if you think things are going off track – you will save time and frustration.
7. Keep checking the quality of the output.
8. Give credit for success and identify the things that made the project run smoothly. Repeat these next time!

The roles people play in meetings

Leader – strengths include energy, determination, initiative, drive, bring people together but MAY get impatient, be domineering and sometimes overreact.

Encourager – strengths include the ability to energise, support and praise others. They don't much like sitting around and will try to move things along, often using humour.

Compromiser – their aim is to maintain harmony within the team. They may be willing to change their own position in order to get a group decision. They are good listeners and tolerant of others.

Summarizer – contribute by clarifying objectives and summarizing conclusions. They are good at dealing with detail and tying up loose ends.

Ideas Person- these are big picture thinkers who get bored with detailed discussions. They love to kick start problem solving but may lose interest after the initial impetus wears off.

Evaluator – they need to think things over before coming to a decision and are very good at evaluating competing proposals. They ensure that the group doesn't rush into making decisions.

Recorder – like to be involved in time keeping, note taking and keeping the group organised. They may check regularly that each team member agrees with the plan and is clear about their responsibilities.

...cont'd

BEWARE being or working with any of the following!

The Autocrat – dominates, interrupts others

The Show off – all talk, no substance

The Butterfly – is always moving to the next subject before finishing the current one

The Aggressor – negative comments about others, no respect for team

The Avoider – no ability to focus on task

The Critic – puts others down, focuses on the negative

The Help Seeker – the victim seeking help

The Self Confessor – inappropriate self disclosure

The Clown – distracts others and unable to get involved with the task

Training

Training doesn't have to be expensive and it is one of the most motivational things you can do. It is good for us all to learn new skills and demonstrates a commitment to the individual. Your customers expect to deal with professional staff and nothing will damage your brand more than contact with offhand, ill-informed employees.

One of the most effective ways to learn is to teach. If you are having to train people to use new products or technology then take responsibility for leading these sessions. Don't hide behind a training manager – it'll be good for your understanding and credibility to demonstrate a detailed knowledge of the subject.

The joy of learning!

There are four stages to learning and we all have to go through them in order to become an expert!

Firstly, unconscious incompetence (you don't know what you don't know).

Secondly, conscious incompetence (you know you don't know!).

Thirdly, conscious competence (you now know you know how but you have to concentrate).

Finally, unconscious competence (you don't even have to think about it anymore!).

A word of caution – every individual will go through each stage at their own pace so never assume everyone is at the same point in their learning journey. Keep checking!

Presentation skills

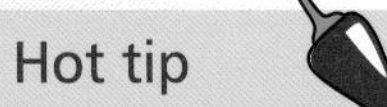

More on perfecting your presentations in **Giving Great Presentations in easy steps** and **Public Speaking in easy steps**

1. You must learn to enjoy, or give the appearance of enjoying, giving presentations! Your audience will respond to your enthusiasm. Smile, make eye contact and speak slowly.

2. Allow yourself plenty of time to prepare your presentation. "It takes one hour of preparation for each minute of presentation time" – Wayne Burgraff.

3. Try to use visual aids to support your message. 55% of what we take in is visual and only 7% is text, so keep words to a minimum! By using visuals, you'll also significantly increase the impact of whatever you say… if not you're only using 38% of the communication medium.

4. Remember that every story has a beginning, middle and end. So should your presentation! Know the main points you must make. Be clear about what you want the audience to remember.

5. The rule of 3 – the brain remembers lists of three, so keep this in mind when planning the content of your presentation! Research has shown that people in the audience remember only 30-40% of speeches and presentation, so be clear before you start what exactly you want the people listening to retain.

6. Take the time to change the material to suit your audience – different groups will want to hear detail that is relevant to them not necessarily a generic message.

7. Be wary of cracking jokes or funny asides. There's no easier way to make your audience feel uncomfortable – and you'll die on your feet if you hear silence when you hoped for laughter!

8 Rehearse, rehearse, rehearse! Try your presentation out in front of a difficult crowd and ask for feedback.

9 Try to anticipate questions that may get asked and have your answers prepared. Take your time to answer on the day so that you can collect your thoughts.

10 Wear plenty of anti-perspirant – dark rings under your shirt are a dead giveaway.

11 Have water close to hand if you worry about drying up (!).

12 Dress appropriately. If you feel good about yourself and your message, you will not go wrong!

13 Relax your shoulders, stand up straight and keep your head centered. Concentrate on breathing slowly and deeply. Speak to the opposite wall so that your voice carries across the room.

14 Don't forget to ask for the order! Make sure you have your audience on your side by the end of the presentation by asking checking questions.

Useful tools

Let's take a little time to cover a few tools you may wish to use to harness your creativity and problem solving capabilities. Marketers rarely work in isolation and team facilitation skills will also serve you well.

Critical thinking is an essential skill of a successful marketer. It is the process we use to reflect on and assess the assumptions that guide our ideas and actions. You need to have the ability to approach situations and opportunities with confidence, perspective, inquisitiveness, and an open mind. Vital to your success is flexibility, the ease with which you are able to adapt, modify or change thoughts, ideas and behaviours.

1. Analyze the problem by breaking it down into parts, study it piece by piece.
2. Judge it against established criteria or standards.
3. Group things or situations together or rank them in order of significance.
4. Find evidence that widens your knowledge.
5. Use logical reasoning to draw conclusions.
6. Predict likely outcomes or consequences.
7. Apply your knowledge to improve other situations.

Want to improve your creative abilities?

Consider keeping an ideas notebook with you at all times and jot down your thoughts as soon as you can. When you review them, you may find nuggets of genius!

Be curious. Ask yourself new questions every day.

Learn about new things. Read widely and with an open mind. Bring ideas from other disciplines into your marketing role.

Avoid getting into a rut with your thinking. Try to develop at least two alternative solutions to every problem. Force yourself to find new perspectives.

Pay attention to what is going on around you and look for similarities and differences in situations and problems.

Be brave! Problem solving means overcoming obstacles so you will need to be persistent and courageous…take risks and have contingency plans.

Know yourself. Understand your own strengths, weaknesses, skills, biases, fears and prejudices.

Have hobbies. This will help you to relax and encourage creativity.

Enjoy yourself! The more fun you have, the easier it will be to harness your creativity.

Socratic Questioning

Based on the work of Socrates, this is a particular type of disciplined questioning that aims to get into the detail of the issue. Used by professionals across many functions, including teachers, psychologists, engineers and marketers, it is a means to get to the heart of a problem or explore complex ideas. It is about using questions to guide learning.

Why do you say that? What exactly does this mean (Clarification)

What could we assume instead? Please explain why/how…? (Probing assumptions)

What would be an example? Why is that happening? (Probing reasons/evidence)

What is another way to look at it? What is the difference between…and..? (Exploring perspectives)

What are you implying? Why is…important? (Exploring consequences/implications)

What does...mean? What else might I ask? (Exploring the question)

Problem solving – the power of 'why'?

Try using the five 'whys' to get to the root of a problem!

State the problem. Ask why. Answer in a statement. Ask why. Answer with another statement. Ask why. Again, write another answer as a statement. Ask why. Another answer. Another why. Your final answer. Now you should be able to identify the real cause of the problem and take preventative action.

Let me give you an example.

Statement: Product literature not available for launch. WHY?

Statement: Not in warehouse. WHY?

Statement: Still at printers. WHY?

Statement: Printers received copy late. WHY?

Statement: Marketer working to different deadline. WHY?

Statement: Project planning sheet hadn't been signed off and circulated. WHY?

cont'd

Get out of that box!

Lateral thinking is the ability to think creatively and approach problems from alternative and often unexpected, angles. It is about throwing away the obvious and freeing yourself of preconceptions.

The following questions may test your lateral thinking skills! Pay close attention to the exact wording of the problem.

What can you hold in your right hand but not your left?

Your left hand, forearm or elbow.

If you were alone in a deserted house at night, and there was an oil lamp, a candle and firewood and you only have one match, which would you light first?

The match.

How many birthdays does a typical woman have?

One.

Is it legal for a man to marry his widow's sister?

No, because he's dead.

A window cleaner is cleaning the windows on the 25th floor of a skyscraper. He falls and slips. He is not wearing a safety harness and nothing breaks his fall yet he suffers no injuries. Why?

He was cleaning the inside of the windows.

Name three consecutive days in English without using the words Tuesday, Thursday or Saturday.

Yesterday, Today, Tomorrow.

A police officer saw a truck driver blatantly going down the wrong way in a one way street. Why did he not try to stop him?

The truck driver was walking.

Mind mapping

The map is not the territory...

Hot tip

Try using a mind map to capture evolving ideas by adding to it every day as you learn more about the subject. It is an effective way of organizing related concepts without having to wade through lots of notes.

...but it's a really good start! Mind mapping is a great technique for presenting complex information in a memorable way. You can start your own mind map by writing the concept in the middle of the page (for instance, "strategic marketing plan") and then link all the elements that contribute to the plan (for example, customer service, sales, distributors, marketing communications). Basically, your mind map is a visual way of explaining a hierarchy. You can make it multi-dimensional, capturing the strategic view and details.

A good mind map makes it easy for the team to see how they each fit into the overall project. It is also a very effective way of ensuring that every function or individual is represented and involved.

There are many mind map software tools available but it's perfectly OK to start with pen and paper!

Brainstorming... a problem shared

This is a group creativity technique which can be used to identify/define problems and/or find solutions.

There are usually roles for a team leader, scribe and team members (between 5 and 10).

Basic ground rules for brainstorming

1. Have a short (5-10 mins) warm-up exercise, which should relax participants.
2. Keep the objective of the session in view during the meeting so people can stay focused.
3. There are no bad ideas and every contribution is valid (and valued!).

4. Make sure everyone knows what the problem is before the meeting starts so that they can mentally prepare themselves.

5. The objective is to capture as many ideas as possible in a relatively short space of time.

6. Every idea needs to be captured by the scribe, preferably where the rest of the team can also see what's on the list.

7. Piggy-back ideas and be creative.

8. Have fun and keep the sessions relatively short.

9. Don't evaluate any contribution until after the brainstorming session.

10. At the end of the meeting, review output and cluster ideas. Agree some kind of priority (top 5) and then evaluate them.

11. Try running the session with everyone standing – it keeps energy levels high!

12. Ensure there are no interruptions or distractions (phones off, door closed, and refreshments at the end).

Rapport

This is about being able to see the world from another's point of view or being on someone else's wavelength.

After all, people are more likely to buy from, support and agree with someone who is like themselves than someone to whom they cannot relate.

It is said that the major elements of rapport are how we look (55%), how we sound (38%) and the words that we use (7%). So the words we use are far less important than the way we say them, or how we look when we say them! You'll often hear someone wail "but it's not what I said!" as their opposite number storms off into the distance… but it is what the other person 'heard', using other visual clues.

So the ability to match breathing rates, maintain eye contact and reflect body language are often seen as signs of building rapport. By being aware of the sub-conscious messages we are receiving and sending out we should be able to build good relationships with those we come into contact with.

How to make a good impression

Make a good impression by dressing well, being on time for appointments and by being friendly. Hand out your business cards to establish a level of professionalism.

Before launching into a sales pitch, spend a few minutes finding some common ground, like sport, hobbies, family, etc.

Mirror and match. If your customer is quietly spoken, lower your own voice.

Both sit or both stand, let your customer lead.

Most people speak at the rate of 150-200 words per minute. If you're speaking with a fast talker, try asking closed questions to keep on track. When speaking with a slow talker, resist the temptation to finish their sentences!

Listen actively. Particularly at the beginning of a meeting let the customer do the majority of the speaking, pay close attention and do not interrupt. Show you are listening by maintaining eye contact and nodding.

Take notes and act on any information or requests. Only make promises you can keep.

Personal marketing

Keep your CV up to date. It makes it much easier to apply for jobs as they appear and is also a good reminder of what you have achieved – each year, you should aim to be adding experiences, skills and qualifications.

Keep an eye on the marketing and business courses your local colleges offer. Often your company will be prepared to sponsor or part fund you.

Network. A great way to learn is from others and an even better way to progress your career is to be recommended for a job – 60-70% of jobs are never advertised and of those jobs gained through networking, around 50% are actually created for the individual!

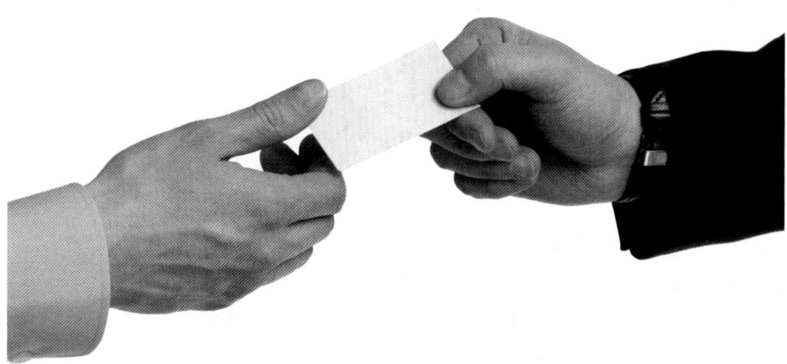

So pick the right events to attend, research the guest list and learn how to keep a conversation going. Give out and collect business cards.

Time for development

No doubt you want to be the best you can be in whatever role you have now or aspire to. Here are some thoughts of areas you might be able to improve on…

1. Imagination – it's a great gift if you can think 'outside the box'. Keep challenging yourself to think of better ways of doing things at work. Give your creativity a work out!

2. Taking criticism – be open, keep calm and stick to facts, be a good critic, manage expectations. Unfair critics get personal, aggressive, criticize your motivation, are negative in their use of language. If you want to know what people think, ask them. Consider 360 degree appraisal – this basically involves people around you (superiors, peers, customers, other functions) providing feedback about your performance.

3. Giving criticism – make it improvement orientated, constructive, kind, based on wanting the best for them. Don't forget that feedback can also be very positive. A simple "well done" or form of recognition for a job well done builds morale.

4. Be adventurous – if you are basically doing the same things in your marketing role year after year, you need to stop and consider.

5. Demonstrate your energy and enthusiasm – people will look to you to be excited about what you're doing. If you don't care, neither will they.

6. Well-informed – make time to scan the business press and marketing magazines for case study information – you'll be surprised how many good ideas you can pick up that will be transferable to your business.

7. Remain open to learning – watch others at work. Be conscious of what they do well. Model it.

8. Use your common sense! Do your best to approach every situation calmly and use logic to work through issues to a satisfactory end point. Try not to get carried away with jargon and hyperbole – more people will understand you and what you're trying to achieve if you keep your thought processes and communications straightforward.

9. Be a great financial manager! Understand financial data and keep your eye on both top line sales and bottom line profit. Pay attention to the detail.

10. Keep this little book close to hand – and recommend it to someone who might appreciate these easily digested nuggets of useful tips!

Summary

1. Learn from those that have gone before you…
2. Have a comprehensive business plan
3. Manage top and bottom lines
4. Have a product worth shouting about.
5. Shout about it in a way that is heard.
6. Experiment with new media but have a contingency plan
7. Have realistic ROI expectations about all forms of marketing communications activity.
8. Weigh up the risks and benefits of any marketing investment.

Heroes and Villains!

There's nothing quite like learning from others' experiences, good or bad. In this chapter we take a look at a number of case studies about companies that have blazed a trail or gone up in smoke.

lastminute.com

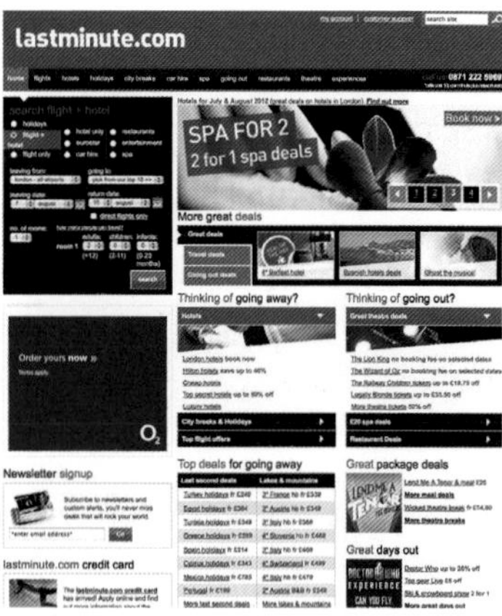

Began life in 1998 and is now one of Europe's premier internet lifestyle websites, selling travel (holidays, flights, hotels etc), experiences (wine tasting, motor racing, beauty treatments etc) and tickets (concerts, theatre, sports events etc).

In 1999, turnover was less than £200,000 and the company made no profit.

By 2000, lastminute.com had sales of £30 million!

Four years later, turnover was £440 million and operating profits were £7.5 million.

Mission – *"To become the number one European e-commerce lifestyle player by delighting our customers with great-value inspiration and solutions."*

Keys to their success –

Focusing on value and service (their customers are cash-rich and time-poor).

Offering an evolving product portfolio (lastminute.com continues to add related products that will enhance the customer's leisure experience).

Making good use of their large organically grown database to drive customer communications (this gives significant competitive advantage as consumers become increasingly wary about sharing information with new companies).

Establishing and maintaining a strong brand (supported by a weekly e-newsletter, word-of-mouth recommendations, an interactive website and their ongoing response to in-house customer satisfaction research).

Growth through acquisition – including, Degrif-Tour (France's biggest online travel company), the Destination Holdings Group (a direct selling international tour operator), Med Hotels, First Option and Gemstone.

Boo.com

Founded in 1998, the company vision was to become the world's first online global sports retail site. Sadly, the company collapsed six months after launching when investors could no longer be persuaded to stump up more funds to meet spiralling costs.

Who was it aiming for?

The target customer group was the fashion-conscious 18-24 year old, interested in prestigious brand leisure and sportswear names.

How would it work?

The aim was to sell clothing via a high tech site which would be capable of recreating the offline shopping experience with a virtual salesperson (Ms Boo), 3D images and helpful advice. It would be the ultimate cool shopping experience.

Where were they?

To begin with, boo.com was available in English (for the UK and US markets), German, Danish, Swedish and Finnish. French, Spanish and Italian were added after the launch. There were two warehouses, one in the US and one in Germany. The company had offices in London, Paris, Munich, New York and Stockholm.

Boo-hoo.com....what went wrong?

High risk global launch strategy

Expensive advertising campaigns yet low brand awareness among internet users. Miniscule brand awareness among non internet users (1.4%)!

Pricing complexity – it proved difficult to manage across different countries.

Sales were disappointing, particularly in the US. Buying customers never appeared in the numbers necessary to generate adequate revenue.

Channel conflict between manufacturers and existing distribution channels vs boo.com

Poor financial control, dodgy metrics and low conversion rates.

...cont'd

Technology that couldn't match the vision – download times, bandwidth restrictions, complexity.

The target customer group were still to see the appeal of mail order, traditionally something for their parents!

Gone but not forgotten…

Ahead of their time, many would say boo.com was a trailblazer for internet retailing. It was Europe's first major dot.com failure, a victim of "cash burn" (high technology and marketing costs). The company may have only lasted for months but e-business goes from strength to strength. Be warned – don't set out without your comprehensive business plan!

Skoda

Why does the Skoda have a heated rear window?

To keep your hands warm!

How do you double the value of a Skoda?

Fill the tank!

What do you call a Skoda with a sun roof?

A skip!

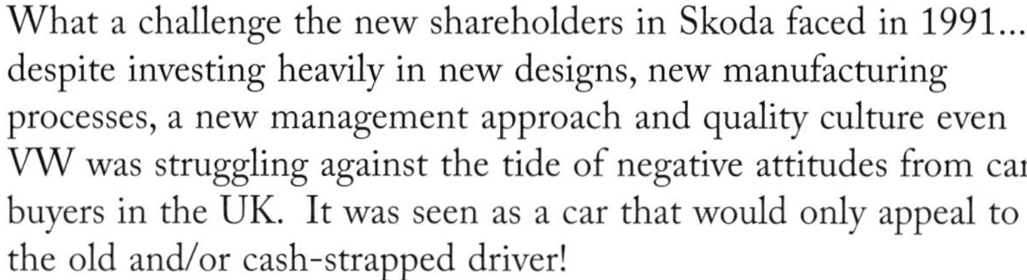
What a challenge the new shareholders in Skoda faced in 1991... despite investing heavily in new designs, new manufacturing processes, a new management approach and quality culture even VW was struggling against the tide of negative attitudes from car buyers in the UK. It was seen as a car that would only appeal to the old and/or cash-strapped driver!

In 2001, VW took complete control of the company. New, improved cars meant higher prices and the time had come to demonstrate why consumers should invest in a Skoda.

Skoda had a strong brand presence in Eastern Europe and was not doing badly in parts of Western Europe. VW decided to back the brand and address the UK market head on with a campaign that gently poked fun at themselves with " The Fabia is a car so good that you won't believe it's a Skoda!"

The 2001 campaign was a winner! Made up of advertising on TV, posters and print; PR and direct mail; and a competition in a well respected car magazine. By mid 2001, there was a waiting list for the Fabia in the UK and other models saw a double digit increase in sales. By 2004, Skoda was seen as a leader in customer satisfaction. The use of humour has also become a tradition in Skoda's campaigns...

Customer perception in the UK has also changed. Now one of the fastest growing brands, significantly more drivers seriously consider buying a Skoda.

DeLorean Motor Company

During the 1970's, Former General Motors exec, John DeLorean decided to build a snazzy European sports car for the US market. His company was based in Belfast, Northern Ireland. A muddy field was transformed into the DeLorean car plant and production of the DMC-12 began in early 1981.

John DeLorean was a flamboyant character who knew cool when he saw it. Surrounded by the rich and famous, he was drawn to the excitement and fast pace of the youth market. The public was as interested in him as his cars.

Great product?

The car looked fantastic! There was nothing like it on the market at the time. A two seater stainless steel car with gull wing doors, the plant produced about 9,000 cars before closing at the end of 1982.

BUT

The car had a reputation for leaking windows and engines that seized. It was not the quickest car on the market by any means, delivering 0-60 in 10.5 seconds! Most importantly, its $25,000 price tag was an issue – expensive for 1981 and $5000 more than its competitor, the Corvette.

Another P!

There was also a political dimension. The UK government had invested heavily in order to regenerate a poor area of Northern Ireland – when sales failed to materialise, further investment stopped.

The final chapter

DeLorean was arrested by the FBI for drug trafficking in October 1982. He was accused of trying to raise money for his car company through drug deals. He was cleared two years later. By then, the car was already history.

Let's Focus on Doug for a minute!

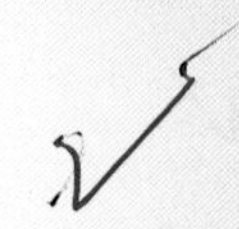

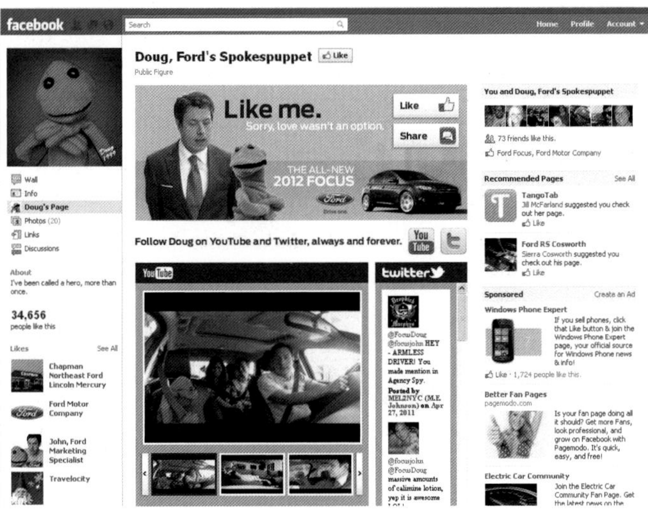

Meet Doug, a bright orange glove puppet, who is the star of a viral campaign run by Ford in 2011.

His mission?

To make the Ford Focus cool in the US.

How?

Doug interacts with the public via Twitter, Facebook and YouTube in a series of unbranded videos. Within one month, there are over 1 million views of his heroic acts, as he prevents a woman from choking, saves a man who has collapsed and foils an armed robbery. Eventually Ford "give" Doug a new Focus to help him continue his work before he takes on a role as the new Ford spokesman.

Doug has a growing number of followers on Facebook and Twitter. His edgy humour and the sophisticated storyline are used to take on the negative perceptions of the Ford Focus in a way which creates buzz and raises awareness.

Softly, softly...

This is a great example of a campaign that doesn't blind the consumer with branding but engages the viewer and keeps them hooked!

Skittles – a dangerous game?

The candy may be pretty, but the Skittles experiment in 2009 with social media marketing certainly wasn't!

In March 2009, the Mars owned Skittles homepage was designed to be an online portal featuring a live Twitter feed. On the same page were links to Facebook, YouTube and Flickr. Skittles didn't filter the results in any way so users could make any comment in any way they wished. Any tweets containing the word 'skittles' immediately appeared on the homepage.

Within two days the strategy had to be dramatically altered. Twitter users had flooded the site with nonsense and abusive comments. What might have been simply a creative use of new technology actually encouraged the Twitter community to turn against them....

Imaginative. Entertaining. Ground breaking. Headline grabbing. All was certainly not lost!

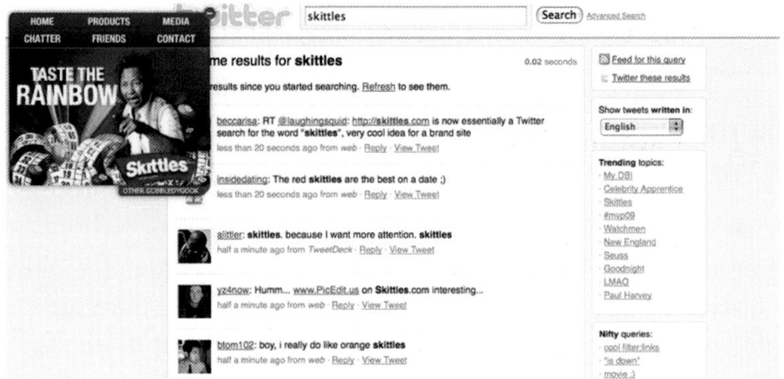

How NOT to FAIL...

1. Know your customers.
2. Know your business.
3. Know your plan.
4. Have sufficient capital.
5. Control your growth.
6. Keep evolving.
7. Understand your cash flow.
8. Watch your bottom line.
9. Price properly.
10. Have the skills that the business needs.
11. Be critical.

Buyer beware!

Many marketers are tempted to find the perfect celebrity to endorse their product. There is the commonly held belief that having a prominent figure on side can significantly enhance your brand attributes.

If celebrity endorsement seems to be what you are looking for, bear in mind that you are looking for a long term relationship – your target market probably wants to see consistency in your approach.

Think creatively about the match between your target audience and your ideal celebrity. Research both with the same diligence.

Celebrity endorsement is only one part of the brand building process. Proceed with caution!

Here are a few examples of the heroes and villains of celebrity endorsement campaigns -

England football player, David Beckham. Endorses Brylcreem, Police sunglasses, Gillette and Vodafone to the tune of £50 million a year. Global role model and superstar.

Manchester United and England football player, Wayne Rooney. Coca Cola was less than happy about his antics off the field which came to media attention in 2006. Dubious role model!

Model, Kate Moss. H&M, Chanel and Burberry dropped her after alleged cocaine misuse in 2005. Now back on track and as high profile as ever.

Golfer, Tiger Woods. Lost Gatorade and AT&T after revelations about his personal life hit the global media in 2009. In addition, Accenture had to bin an entire campaign.

Singer, Madonna. In 1989, Pepsi dropped their campaign when "Like a Prayer" was released simultaneously as both a single and the soundtrack to the drinks advert. Madonna's controversial video caused such an outcry that the ad had to be shelved.

Athletes, Dan O'Brien & Dave Johnson. Reebok invested $25 million on an ad campaign in the US. Don failed to qualify for the 1992 Olympics and Dave came home with one bronze medal. Four years later, Dan O'Brien won the gold in Atlanta (but the campaign was well and truly over by then!).

Check before you leap!

1. Is there a connection between your brand and the celebrity?
2. Is the celebrity credible?
3. Is your celebrity bigger than your brand?
4. Could you "create" your own spokesperson/character?
5. Is the endorsement cost effective? How will you measure your ROI?
6. Can you identify an emerging celebrity (rather than an established one) who fits your brand values?
7. Can you get out of the agreement if it backfires?
8. Take out "Death and Disgrace" insurance to protect your campaign investment!

Summary

- Learn from those that have gone before you…keep up to date with the marketing press and study current case studies.
- Have a comprehensive business plan – from this will come your marketing plan, which in turn will flow into all the other plans around the company.
- Manage your top and bottom lines. You need sales and profit in order to succeed! Ensure you have regular access to vital financial information.
- Have a product worth shouting about! Getting new customers costs five times as much as retaining your existing customers so build customer service into your marketing plans.
- Shout about it in a way that is heard. Don't try to be an expert in everything however – bring in suppliers if you can and learn from them.
- Experiment with new media but have a contingency plan. Mistakes are a healthy part of learning but don't leave yourself unnecessarily exposed!
- Have realistic ROI expectations about all forms of marketing communications activity.
- Weigh up the risks and benefits of any marketing investment. Then go for it!

"If you wish in this world to advance
Your merits you're bound to enhance,
You must stir it and stump it,
And blow your own trumpet,
Or, trust me, you haven't a chance."
W.S.Gilbert

Resources

PEST Analysis

Porters 5 Forces

SWOT Analysis

Ansoff's Product/Market Matrix

The 4Ps

Boston Matrix

Writing a Brief

Writing a Press Release

Use SMART objectives

Customer Matrix

Call Centre Basic Guide

Planning Tools – Sales Stats

Outline Marketing Plan

Your Business Plan

PEST Analysis

Define your market
Political
Economic
Socio-demographic
Technological

CUSTOMER SEGMENT SALES ANALYSIS

	Quantity	Total Sales Values	Average Value	% Gross Margin	Total Sales or Gross Margin
Segment 1					
Segment 2					
Segment 3					
Segment 4					
Segment 5					

DISTRIBUTOR SALES ANALYSIS

	Quantity	Total Sales Values	Average Value	% Gross Margin	Total Sales or Gross Margin
Distributor 1					
Distributor 2					
Distributor 3					
Distributor 4					
Distributor 5					

Outline Marketing Plan

Project Name:

Date:

Written by:

Executive Summary

Situation Analysis

The macro environment, the market (past, present, future), competition, customer analysis, product analysis, distribution/channel analysis.

Own Product Definition

Strengths and weaknesses, benefits to consumer

Competitors

Direct and Indirect
Competitor A (strengths and weaknesses)
Competitor B (strengths and weaknesses)

Cont'd

Product comparison

Price and performance

Customer Segmentation

Demographics, lifestyles, product/service usage

Communications Strategy

Different marketing messages per different segment

Product Launch Plan

Pricing, sales forecast, timescales, budget, promotion

Cont'd

PR Strategy

Timeline, major events, contingency

Advertising

Budget, timelines, media, metrics

Promotional Plan

Direct, indirect, budget, metrics

Packaging

Presentation, pricing, strategy, fulfilment, translation issues

Cont'd

Pricing

Strategy, policies

Distribution

Strategy, channels, international requirements (pricing, presentation etc)

Metrics

Sales, profit, volume, ROI
Daily, weekly, monthly, annually.

Marketing Schedule

Activity by timeline/phase

Your Business Plan

Mission Statement

Clearly state your company's long-term mission.

– Try to use words that will help direct the growth of your company, but be as concise as possible.

The Team

List CEO and key management by name. Include previous accomplishments to show that these are people with a record of success.

Summarize number of years of experience in this field.

Market Summary

Summarize your market in the past, present, and future.

–Review those changes in market share, leadership, players, market shifts, costs, pricing, or competition that provide the opportunity for your company's success.

Opportunities

Identify problems and opportunities.

–State consumer problems, and define the nature of product/ service opportunities that are created by those problems.

Business Concept

Summarize the key technology, concept, or strategy on which your business is based.

Competition

Summarize the competition. Outline your company's competitive advantage.

Goals and Objectives

List five-year goals. State specific, measurable objectives for achieving your five-year goals.

– List market-share objectives.

– List revenue/profitability objectives.

Financial Plan

Outline a high-level financial plan that defines your financial model and pricing assumptions.

– This plan should include expected annual sales and profits for the next three years.

– Use several slides to cover this material appropriately.

Resource Requirements

List requirements for the following resources:

– Personnel

– Technology

– Finances

– Distribution

– Promotion

– Products

– Services

Risks and Rewards

Summarize the risks of the proposed project and how they will be addressed.

Estimate expected rewards, particularly if you are seeking funding.

Key Issues

Near term

– Identify key decisions and issues that need immediate or near-term resolution.

– State consequences of decision postponement.

Long term

– Identify issues needing long-term resolution.

– State consequences of decision postponement.

If you are seeking funding, be specific about any issues that require financial resources for resolution.

Index

R

S

T

W